SEASONAL DISORDER

SEASONAL DISORDER

Ranger Tales
from Glacier National Park

PAT HAGAN

Johnson Books
BOULDER

Published by Johnson Books, a division of Big Earth Publishing,
3005 Center Green Drive, Suite 220, Boulder, Colorado 80301.
E-mail: books@bigearthpublishing.com
www.johnsonbooks.com

Cover design: Peter Streicher, shushu design
Composition: Eric Christensen

9 8 7 6 5 4 3 2 1

Library of Congress Cataloging-in-Publication Data
Hagan, Pat.
     Seasonal disorder: ranger tales from Glacier National Park / Pat Hagan.
        p. cm.
     ISBN 1-55566-374-5
   1. Hagan, Pat. 2. Park rangers–Montana–Glacier National Park–Biography. 3. United
States. National Park Service–Officials and employees–Biography. 4. Natural History–
Montana–Glacier National Park. 5. Glacier National Park (Mont.) I. Title.
     SB481.6.H34A3 2006
     363.6'8092–dc22   2006004138

Printed in the United States

Contents

"Anybody who takes this book seriously will be shot!"
—Edward Abbey, *Hayduke Lives!*

"The truth is a precious commodity;
therefore we shall be economical with its use."
—Mark Twain, *Following the Equator*

"Hmmm? Do you think the Ed Abbey quote is too much?"
—Pat Hagan, Pondering at the Computer

Introduction

Montana has been described as the "Last Best Place." That is true for a variety of reasons: the warmth of the people, the stunning and varied landscape, and the fact that it still has no sales tax all make Montana a special place. People come from the four corners of the globe to experience what this land has to offer, like rugged mountains, grizzly bears, and old Mom and Pop stores that still sell globes with four corners. It is an extraordinary place, and within its borders lies what could be the most beautiful land this side of heaven: Glacier National Park.

John Muir, the noted naturalist and founder of one of America's lesser national parks, Yosemite, said that Glacier National Park "has the greatest care-killing scenery in the world ... and it can make you truly immortal." Sadly, shortly after saying this, Muir died. But, inspired by his words, I've tried to come up with a safer quote, one that doesn't tempt fate too much. I say, "Glacier National Park is so beautiful that it will mess you up for the rest of your life."

Years ago, I came to Glacier, and it messed me up big time. I was hired by the National Park Service as a naturalist or "Interpreter," and according to the job description, I was to "frolic and make merry in leafy glades." Not too many jobs allow a person to do that and still wear a badge. Understandably, I fell in love with my work, and I wouldn't trade my job with anyone, with the possible exception of Bill Gates. No, come to think of it, I wouldn't switch even with him.

Glacier National Park covers 1 million acres. There is much to explore and so much to see, you can't do it all in one season. Naturally, I kept coming back to hike and explore this park, summer after summer, year after year. Suddenly I realized that this "seasonal job" *was my life.* I understood that I was afflicted with a "seasonal disorder." Three months in Glacier were more important than the other nine months anywhere else. (I realize that some people suffer from a depression known as "seasonal affective disorder," or SAD syndrome, and they may take exception with my politically incorrect choice for a title. So, from the bottom of my heart, I'd like to say to these people, "lighten up"–sheeze!)

My seasonal disorder isn't unique. Tens of thousands are similarly afflicted. These people are like the swallows of Capistrano; they return to their favorite parks annually, like clockwork. Some are rangers like me who work seasonally in the park that inspires them the most, be it Teton, Yellowstone, or Denali. It is my opinion that Glacier has messed up the most lives. For example, I know plenty of people who have given well over twenty-five years of seasonal service there. I know a few with over thirty-five seasons, and one man has worked seasonally in Glacier for about forty-five years. He's really sick—yet strangely happy and energetic.

That's what this seasonal disorder is all about: summer in Paradise, for as long as you can make it last. I was so taken with this ice-sculpted wilderness that my family and I moved to live on Glacier's border, got longer working periods, and extended my season. After a hard week of hiking the trails, I'd spend my weekend relaxing by hiking more trails. I also read a lot of books on Glacier. As a trail guide, I needed to be informed or, in my case, pretend to be informed. I read about the park's history, botany, mycology, and mammalogy, and for a little spice along the path, I'd have a few anecdotes at the ready.

Being born and raised in Montana, I have read a lot of Montana authors, and I feel I understand what motivated and inspired so many. This rugged land can make you do crazy things. In my case, I was driven to write. I didn't have a lot of free time, so I wrote sporadically. I wrote when I wasn't watching my two children, working in the park or at my wife's diner, or adding to my roadkill collection. I wrote only when I had the time. I wrote very little. It is said that you should write about what you know, so I wrote even less. But what did make it to paper was about Glacier National Park.

I've always liked poetry. So I wrote many poems about Glacier in the style I knew best. Then a friend pointed out that Glacier doesn't have any places named Nantucket or Regina. Without those two place-names, my poetry was shot. So I decided to write prose. Yet the market for "Glacier books" seemed to be totally and utterly saturated. There were lots of Glacier books already in print. How could I fit in? How could I write something new? I couldn't, so I just started to plagiarize others (but only the really good stuff).

Needless to say, the plagiarism route to success didn't work. I had to come up with a new method of writing that was more me and less of the other authors. Help and inspiration came in an unexpected way. It came not at a writing desk but at a poker table.

One night, during a particularly tense game, I reviewed the cards in my hand. Respectable, I thought, but my steely-eyed opponent kept confidently adding to the kitty and raising the stakes. I couldn't take the pressure. I looked at my cards, grimaced, and folded. As my friend smiled and showed me her cards, I was shocked. She didn't have anything in her hand, and she beat my full house! "I was bluffing," she said simply. Bluffing. It was a valuable lesson. It's OK to bluff. She had just given me advice that would get me through my writing, through the writer's block, through the dry spells.

The lesson: "I don't need facts to write a book—I'll just make stuff up and pretend it happened." Just omit the facts and add a dash of fancy in its place. So, for those looking to learn about Glacier, I'd like to apologize in advance. I'm not writing as an emissary of the Park Service. I'm not representing the Park Service at all. They're an honorable bunch, and I'm not. I'm bluffing. I'm writing for fun. I'm not bothering with the "facts" because that would take "time" and "research," and, frankly, I'm not going to put forth the "effort."

I'm too lazy. So, if you're looking to learn something about Glacier, I need to be honest and say: There are no sage words, no deep philosophical concepts, and no firmer thighs in two weeks. There's not a lot of truth to be found here. It's a collection of lies. Except that part about John Muir. Glacier truly does have some great scenery. Better than Yosemite, anyway.

The First Trip

In the car chase of life, my sister Malady is a fruit stand, frequently in the wrong place at the wrong time. Malady, as a youngster, always had a "fragile disposition." As a little girl, things like fishing poles, musty tents, or a can of beans would throw her into a "fretful state." Luckily, after years of therapy, that young girl has matured into a full-grown "nervous wreck." Apparently, her therapist feels Malady is repressing some memories related to the whole family going camping because she said her first "real" vacation was her trip to Fiji, a calm tropical paradise where a couple can relax and young children are not allowed unless previously chloroformed or otherwise sedated. The therapist, who is seeing all twelve members of my family (volume discount), asked me to be "sensitive" about her state.

"Sensitive," I told the therapist, as he lay upon the couch with an icepack on his head, "just happens to be my middle name" (the first being "Not" and the last being, "At all").

Later, back at my parents' house, I gently reminded Malady that her first "real" vacation that I recall with any clarity was up at Glacier.

"Malady, surely you remember all those times the whole family went camping up in Glacier?" She winced and shuddered, and one of her eyes started to twitch. The other eye just had a vacant look.

"C'mon, Malady! You remember! That time, when I was six at Two Medicine. Dad, Mom, Mary Ellen, Jim, Danny Boy, Mary Katherine, David, Janice Marie, Marilyn Celeste, you, me, and little Chris. You know, 'The Whole Fam Damily.'"

I looked Malady right in the eye, the one not twitching, and continued, "you remember ..." I took a fishing rod down from its resting place on the wall and handed it to her to trigger a memory. She held it in both hands. She stared at it for a moment, and then, as I expected, memories came flooding back. Both eyes rolled back into her head, and she stiffened like an oak plank and fell over backward. Horrified, I quickly went over and very gently, very carefully, grabbed the fishing rod. Luckily, it was okay. Then, I bent over her and slapped her face, not to bring her back to consciousness, but because she almost broke a rod that held so many memories.

Ah, Glacier Park! I was young, and my recollections may be a bit muddled, but they're coming back. (The therapist is quite pleased with my progress.) I remember all the family sitting around the campfire, telling tales of fierce animals and ghost stories late into the night. The smell of smoke. The mountains, the lakes, and all the critters. My first vacation into Glacier National Park, August 1970.

Back in the "good ol' days," as everyone in our family, except Malady, likes to call them, we would load up our trusty wood-paneled wagon with all the provisions needed for a week of quality family time outdoors. Dad was in charge of logistics and provisions. Into the back of the old car went the tents, sleeping bags, coolers packed with food, extra clothing, rain gear, binoculars, and, of course, Dad's barbeque grill. Whatever couldn't be crammed into the car was strapped onto the luggage rack, but luckily that was just the older kids. Mom was in charge of smaller details: personal items, like a change of underwear. We all had a change of undies, but I didn't much care for Dave's, and he thought mine were too tight.

Fitting into the car was kind of like a frat house stunt where all those kids pile into a phone booth. Being the runt of the family, I easily found a spot in the 2-inch gap between Malady and my big brother Dave, way in the back of the wagon. It is a six-hour trip from my hometown of Anaconda to Glacier, and a kid my age could get easily bored unless there was some amusement. Malady was an easy teasing target.

My favorite car game to play with my sister Malady was called "I'm not touching you." Our family's road trip mantra was "Keep your hands to yourself" (and, to a lesser extent, "Don't make me pull this car over!"). I would point my finger at her face, about a quarter of an inch away. There my finger hovered, relentlessly, ever-present in front of her face. I'd say in a high, raspy voice, "I'm not touching you. I'm not touching you." She would wiggle and squirm, trying to get more distance from my finger, and would sometimes be able to increase her distance from my finger to about half an inch.

But I'd continue to point and say "I'm not touching you." I was a good boy and would "keep my hands to myself." Then, WHAM! right in my arm. I turned 180 degrees to see my brother Dave smirking and holding up his fist, saying, "I *am* touching you. I *am* touching you." Dave was a bad boy who couldn't keep his hands to himself.

It was a long trip to Glacier. It was overcast, with occasional snow flurries, typical August weather. Dad had to pull over a couple of times, but it wasn't behavior-related, unless you consider shivering a behavior. It was just to thaw out the luggage rack kids (rotisserie-style) over the barbeque grill.

After hours of travel, teasing, not touching, punching, and thawing, we finally made it to our destination: the Two Medicine Valley of Glacier National Park. The valley has stunning mountains that strain to touch the sky and lakes of cobalt blue teeming with trout. Compared to other valleys, it was relatively undiscovered. A small number of campers saw our wagon pull into the campground, loaded with small tots inside and teen-cicles outside. Apparently, it was enough to shock them into leaving. We had the entire campground to ourselves.

The first order of business was to gather firewood and pitch tents. Dad would take care of the tents, Mom would take care of the cooking, and the ten kids would scour the forest for firewood. The brood went running willy-nilly, pell-mell, hell-bent for leather into the trees. The more agile of us ran between them to gather the wood.

I returned with an armload of wood and palms loaded with slivers. I milled about, looking around and watching Mom cook. I waited hungrily with baited breath. Why I was picking at the bait, I don't recall. But I was excited! I was camping and hungry.

After we did our chores and Mom and Dad got the camp in order, Mom served up a fantastic meal of "weenie-o-bean" on cold metal trays. The trays would get hot under the beans, and we'd all warm our hands. Everything tastes great while camping, which, come to think of it, probably explains the bait.

After washing up, Dave said he'd take Malady and me fishing. Mom was worried that in the diminishing light and with a new moon I was sure to get the lure snagged in some willows, some brush, or some of Malady's hair. But Dave winked at my mom and said not to worry about any snags. He grabbed the rod and put some ugly, horrible thing on the end of the line that looked a lot like a tiny, mangled mouse. I thought the lure was worthless, but Dave explained as we walked that fish love mice.

"Why, sometimes, fish will come right up out of the water and walk on their little fins right into a meadow. They go into the dry grass and scoop up the field mice and bop them on the head and bring them back to the water so they can gobble them up and wash them down at the same time." As a young boy Dave had an ability to lie that would have made any seasoned politician envious.

Though it was only a short walk to the lake, there was still some potential that boredom's hand might fall upon me. For entertainment, I decided to point at Malady: "I'm not touching you." WHAM! Right in the arm, again! Being so far from Mom and Dad seemed to make Malady bolder. She punched with agonizing accuracy into the bruise Dave had previously established during the car ride. My boredom quickly dissipated.

Once we got to the lake, Dave again told us his walking fish tales. To prove his point, he reached back with the rod and cast the mouse lure into a meadow a few feet from the lake. I watched the mouse sail through the air and land among the tall, dry grasses. Being young and naive, I carefully watched the area between the meadow and the lake to see if any fish would come ambling out of the water toward the mouse lure. I half expected the older fish to come out stooped and with little walking canes. Again, I waited with bated breath, but this time I spelled it correctly.

I waited, but nothing happened. I began to think that Dave was playing a joke on me, and so I said, "Reel the mouse in; I think it's too far away, and the fish don't know it's there. ..." Dave grinned down at me and nodded. He reeled the mouse in, and I swear, some shadow in the brush and trees moved as if ready to pounce on the lure.

"Did you see that!?" I said, with eyes like saucers (I didn't bother to use my mouth). Apparently neither Malady's nor Dave's night vision was as good as mine. "Did a fish come out of the water?" Malady said.

"No. There's something up in the tree *and* down in the bushes. Cast again, quick!"

He cast the lure again. He wasn't watching where the lure landed; rather, he was just watching Malady and me. But this time, as Dave reeled in the mouse lure, a great horned owl silently peeled off the branch of a cottonwood and pounced upon the lure. It hit with silent wings flapping, again and again, up and down. Then it flew up into the air, carrying the tiny lure right over us. Dave gave a small tug on the line, and the lure popped out of the owl's talons. The owl continued on out of sight as if nothing remarkable had happened. Dave, Malady, and I just stood there, our mouths agape.

Dave recovered quickly and put his political skills into practice. "You know, fish love mice; but so do many a nocturnal creature such as skunks, bears, but especially owls. I knew there was an owl in that tree, but I just wanted to show you two that you can catch any number of critters with one of these lures. Let's do it again."

With the patience of Zen masters, we cast the lure out again and again for the owl, but to no avail. It just wouldn't strike. After about five casts, we gave up and headed back to camp. The patience of the Zen master is much shorter when you are young.

Back at the camp, we told everyone about fishing for owls. I reminded Dave that there were two "things" out there: one in the tree and one in the bushes. We knew one was an owl, but what was the other? Dave dismissed it all and started to tell the tale of how with each cast, the owl would come down and strike the lure. With each retelling of the story the owl seemed to grow a little larger, and if it hadn't been so dark, we could have seen Dave's nose growing, too.

After a long discourse on all creatures nocturnal, sleep began its descent upon the camp. Dave and the others headed to their tents. I was to share a tent with Malady, who seemed a bit reluctant, especially after the car ride. She was always a bit fragile, and within the confines of a tent I could actually hear her nerves audibly jangle. We had the tent nearest the outhouse, about 30 feet away, in case the jangling affected her bladder in the middle of the night.

I wasn't particularly sleepy just yet. I wanted to go fishing for owls and told Malady that I'd be back to the tent after she was asleep. She gave me the evil eye, suspecting that I was up to no good. After a while, she climbed into the open pup tent and into her sleeping bag. But she kept her head outside the opening—just in case.

Alone, I headed with the pole back to the lake shore. Fatigue worked its way into my body, but I fought like a real six year old. At the lake, I cast parallel to the shoreline, hitting just a few feet away from the water (I still use this fishing method as an adult, but not on purpose). I cast several times in different areas, hoping to see the fish or owls come out for the lure, but no critter ever showed. Then I remembered the bush. Right before the owl had pounced on the lure, there had been some rustling in a nearby bush. In the gathering darkness, I wasn't too sure which bush it had been; everything looked the same. I spent a lot of time uselessly casting the mouse lure into bushes. It never snagged on anything, and I figured out why Dave had winked at Mom earlier. This lure wouldn't snag a thing without a hook.

After I spent a long time casting about, fatigue crashed into my six-year-old body. One minute I was fishing for owls; the next minute I knew I needed to head for the tent and some well-deserved sleep. Forgetting even to reel in the lure, I headed straight for the tent, dragging the mouse through the dry grass on the line 30 feet behind me.

I suppose if I had been a little more awake, I would have heard more than the mouse lure rustle in the dry grass.

Looking back on it, it sure made a lot of noise and even got snagged a couple of times. But, as it was, I was just a sleepy little kid clutching a pole and towing a mouse 30 feet behind.

I went to the tent, but then remembered that I needed to use the biffy prior to climbing into the sack. So off I went toward the outhouse—still clutching the pole and dragging the lure right to the opening of the tent where Malady's head rested upon a pillow. Just before I opened the outhouse door, I heard Malady give a little scream. I looked back blurry-eyed and saw an ugly cat standing right at the opening of our tent holding the mouse lure in its mouth. An ugly black cat with tail held jauntily in the air. The tail appeared to have whitish stripes, but my mind reasoned that it was just the moonlight reflecting off it. Even though there was no moon.

I suppose if Malady hadn't screamed, all would have been well. If she hadn't screamed, I would have just thought nothing of the ugly cat. It would have just walked away. If she hadn't screamed, we could have kept the old canvas pup tent and the sleeping bags. But, as it was, she did scream, and ugly cats don't like it one bit when you scream right in their faces. Skunks can be that way.

Well, that skunk defended itself the only way it knew how. It let fly with a jet of super-sulfur stink, hitting Malady squarely in the face, which caused her to stop screaming and start heaving up her weenie-o-bean dinner. At that point the various family members emerged from their tents, yelling, asking questions, staggering about in the underwear they'd been assigned, and holding their noses. This chaos caused the skunk to think it had been ambushed and surrounded by a deranged and disturbed family, which was ridiculous because my family didn't surround it. It then sought the closest possible refuge, which, of course, was my sister's tent. With the skunk entering the tent, my sister shot out like a cannonball, leaving a roadrunner-like cloud of dust.

We never would have found her, but once the dust settled, there was still a faint trail of weenie-o-bean leading to the lake. Given the chill in the air, the temperature of the lake, and Malady's fragile disposition, I was surprised to see her submerged up to her armpits and scouring her face. She could be tough under the right circumstances.

That really was the end of the adventure. We had to get rid of the tent and a couple of sleeping bags, and we almost got rid of Malady. She scrubbed up as best she could and eventually rubbed off the stink, until she got to the point at which she just smelled like week-old roadkill on a hot, humid day.

"Hey, Malady! Earth to Malady!" I yelled at the comatose form of my sister in my most sensitive voice. "C'mon, wake up. Cowboy it up."

"Fiji. Your first vacation was Fiji?" I said to my sister. "How could you forget that trip to Two Medicine and this here fishing pole?" She fixed her eyes on the pole and then her eyes just rolled up and she fell back on the floor with a dull thunk. I guess she still has that fragile disposition and poor memory. I don't see how she could forget that particular trip or the ride home back to Anaconda. She was all alone on the roof rack.

The Anti-Glacier: Anaconda

They say that opposites attract. While this cliché isn't true in all cases, it's true enough in my life. For example, I'm personally drawn to intelligent, vibrant people who smell nice. And that wacky cliché is the very reason I find Glacier National Park so magnificent and pristine. You see, I grew up in the opposite of Glacier, an area of Montana known for its contamination and grime. A town that polluted all that was downwind and killed all plant life for miles. The anti-glacier, the exact opposite of Glacier: Anaconda, Montana.

Don't get me wrong. I'm very proud of where I grew up. The people of that town show a character seldom seen anymore. They know how deep their roots go and how their foundations were built upon the backs of their grandfathers, how those men struggled and toiled through arsenic and other toxins at the smelter just to make the lives of their

grandchildren better than the lives they knew. The people of
Anaconda are tough. They have character–and in addition,
they are also completely immune to arsenic poisoning.

The town itself was founded by an Irish immigrant by the
name of Marcus Daly. It was said that Daly had a "nose for
ore" and could smell precious metals hundreds of feet under-
ground. (He was very popular at beaches, where he'd get
down on all fours and sniff the sand, beeping along the
shoreline, locating lost earrings and pocket change.)About
1880, Daly built the smelter city of Anaconda, and because of
his Irish heritage and his strong work ethic, hired lots of
Yugoslavs to work his smelter. Many Irish people came to
protest the hiring of cheap Slavic labor, so Daly hired them
too (at half the price). The Irish and the Yugoslavs, or, to use
the politically correct terms of the day, "harps" and "bohunks,"
got along splendidly. They would go to company picnics,
drink beer, and have fistfights. It is a proud tradition that con-
tinues to this very day. Yes, they got along splendidly–unless
they were together.

My dad was born in Anaconda, and grandpa came when he
was but a babe. My great-grandfather was a charter member
of the smelter men's union (until the concept caught on, he
was the only member). All families worked at the smelter, or,
as they said, "on the hill" for the Anaconda Company, or
simply "the Company." The Anaconda way of life was to work
on the "hill" for the "Company" until you "died."

The Company was more than just a provider of jobs. It
brought many of the citizens closer together through
company housing. The Company knew that the men would

be too tired from a shift on the hill to be troubled with taking care of a lawn after work. So, in order to keep the men fresh, the Company houses came with very small lawns with just enough soil to grow a dandelion or two. One could actually trim the lawn with toenail clippers. The houses themselves were quite small and very close together. An aspiring inventor once visited Anaconda and was so inspired by the size and grandeur of the houses that he went on to invent the refrigerator box. One could go to a neighbor's house and borrow a cup of sugar and never leave one's own home. Yes, things were close. To walk between houses, it was first necessary to butter one's suit to ease the friction.

Religion played an important role in Anaconda. It was a large Catholic community; families tended to be large and fruitful and ready to multiply. I came from a small family with only ten children. Mom said she could have had more children, but then she found out what was causing them, so there are only ten of us. The Company even worked its way into our prayers. It was tradition that we were hauled by our ears into church and said our daily prayers and gave our (Marcus) Daly thanks.

The Company stood as our testament to hard work. It was our very own rock of Gibraltar. It would be there as long as we continued to work; it would be there as long as we were fruitful and kept up the demand for labor. Decade after decade, the smelter's stack belched out smoke as ore was turned into fine copper. Personally, I never heard the stack burp, but that was the accepted way of describing it. My great-grandfather, grandfather, dad, and all my older siblings were employed on the hill. My uncle had the special job of keeping track of the honorable politicians on the payroll. I say "honorable" because in those days, once the Company bought politicians—they *stayed* bought.

I would have worked on the hill too. Several times I slipped my application under the personnel door but never received a reply. I thought that it was due to some stringent hiring requirement like reading or math. But alas, the sad truth was that after about 100 years, the Company ran out of gas, and the stack quit belching. The Company had been taken over by another company that pioneered the concept of out-sourcing. The Anaconda Company, as our family knew it, was no more. All over town, family traditions came to a halt. If it weren't for beer, Lord knows what would have happened.

Thousands of people were now out of work. The town's economy was in a serious slump, except for the bars: they were doing fine. People of lesser character would have packed it all in and quit, abandoned the town, and sought employment elsewhere. But the people of Anaconda have character; they have backbone. The citizens lived in a "can-do city" with a "never-say-die attitude." "Where there is a will, there's a way" was a frequently heard motto of the people. In fact, the city commissioners held an emergency meeting, and a Cliché Committee was immediately formed to come up with these upbeat slogans to keep citizen morale at a high level.

Undeterred by the smelter closure and feeling the optimism of the Cliché Committee, the Irish and the Yugoslavs got together, drank beer, and punched one another. It was during this time that the people of Anaconda decided to take this negative situation and put a positive spin on things, take issues other communities would consider liabilities and move them over to the asset column. For instance, many people did move out, and a few homes were available. With no real industry, it was questionable if people would move into such a depressed hamlet. But real estate agents put out enticing advertisements that said, "Buy one house; get your second house free!"

Another example comes from one of the smelters by-products. Just on the east side of town, there is what looks like a jet black mountain of sand. This sand is actually slag, which is a substance like obsidian; actually, it is more like obsidian slivers. A mountain of tiny black shards of glass splinters—*now there's a tourist attraction!* "Come to Anaconda and walk in our slag!" But someone with vision said, "Hey, let's take the slag and put it into pits and we'll build a golf course around the pits—You know, black sand traps!" And with the slag, that is just the tip of the iceberg. If ever a movie were to be made about a nomadic people who traveled endless miles across jet black sand, I assure you the movie would be made in Anaconda. This town just won't go away.

By now Anaconda should be a historical footnote. A town abandoned by its citizens after the collapse of the Company. But it's still there. So are many of the families. They knew jobs would one day return. Sometime in the not-too-distant future, grandchildren of smeltermen would be employed, probably by the federal government as part of the Environmental Protection Agency or a Superfund cleanup crew.

Even though Anaconda has been home to my family for generations, I felt a magnetic tugging pulling me north toward

Brother Bear

They say you can pick your friends and you can pick your nose, but you can't pick your friend's nose. I have tested this cliché—it isn't true. I have picked my friend's nose. She retaliated with a resounding slap. But too late—I picked. There is almost no end to what you can pick, but, alas, with family, you're stuck. Picking is not an option.

If I were able to choose my big brother, he would have turned out like Wally on *Leave It to Beaver*. My chosen big brother would teach me about life, love, philosophy, art, and fishing while saying "gosh" a whole lot. He would read me stories in a big warm chair in front of a fire after making me a hot cocoa. At night, if I was scared, he would comfort me and sing me a lullaby until I drifted off into sleepy-land. That's the type of big brother I'd *choose*. But I was stuck with Dave.

If Dave weren't my brother, I would have considered him the neighborhood bully. Of course, Dave was more than just a bully; there were many facets to his personality. Sometimes he'd take some time off from his "bully" role to engage in a completely different "know-it-all-fibber" role. Looking back, I guess he had just the two facets. Bully or know-it-all, but he couldn't do both at the same time.

Dave never said "Hi!" to me. Too much verbiage. Rather, he'd stroll into a room and punch me in the arm. Not some generalized, random, center-of-mass blow; no, Dave hit the arm with years of honed practice and never failed to hit, with pinpoint accuracy, that really sensitive spot low on the shoulder that would leave a big bruise. He was always punching me in the arm or thumping me on the chest. I still have a slight depression in my sternum that conforms exactly to Dave's middle finger. Frequently, he'd hold me down, kneel on my arms, and thump that finger repeatedly into my chest. It wasn't much fun, but I'd laugh. Oh, I'd laugh until ... I stopped. Once the laughter subsided, I could count on Dave to quit thumping within about forty-five minutes or so. Then he'd let me up, and I'd go a few paces. He'd tackle me, and the process would begin anew. I was lucky to get away with just a thumping; sometimes he'd dangle saliva. I hated that one, but at least I wore glasses.

One of the biggest thrills in Dave's life was to scare the scat out of siblings. Shrieks of terror were like some elixir Dave craved like a junkie. All too frequently, I was the sole target of his scare tactics. Dave raised some pranks to the level of diabolical genius. Once, after seeing a movie with Dracula, the wolf man, the mummy, and the blob, Dave took it upon himself to see if gravity was a constant or merely a law that could be suspended.

This, I recall distinctly, was shortly after Halloween. On Halloween he went trick-or-treating dressed as a gorilla. He bought an ape mask and matching gloves. I remember telling him he could just go out and trick-or-treat; he'd look the same, with or without the mask. That remark earned me a good thumping—drool included at no extra charge. But I digress.

Dave had pre-recorded all these raspy, nasty, evil hissing sounds on cassette tape and placed the tape player under my bed. He had a long extension cord snaked, out of sight, along three walls, to an outlet right next to his bed. He pretended to be sleeping with his back toward me when he slyly plugged in the tape recorder. The eerie sounds came in low at first and then started to grow. The monsters from the movie that previously existed just in my imagination now had receipts to show they owned real estate directly under my bed. First, I pulled the covers over my head, but due to lack of oxygen and a dinner that included beans, that didn't last. I sat bolt upright in bed. "Dave! Do you hear that?!" He casually rolled over, unplugged the extension cord, and feigned listening to a now silent room. "No," he said innocently, "I don't hear anything. Go back to sleep, you little creep, or I'll have to punch you." At this threat, I nervously snuggled down into the covers, waiting to hear the ghostly sounds. Dave rolled over and got ready to plug in the tape recorder—but not too soon, not too soon.

After long, agonizing minutes of waiting and waiting for the ghoulish chorus to begin, sleep finally started to overtake me. As my eyelids fluttered and sleep started to descend, Dave plugged in the tape recorder again.

"Mom! Dad! Monsters!" Cries of help to my parents didn't alleviate the situation; they just told me to go to sleep, which I was fine with, until I realized they meant back in my own bed. While I was out of our bedroom pleading my case to Mom and Dad, Dave crept from his bed, turned up the volume, and slunk back into his own bed. Mom came into my room and looked under the bed to assure me there were no monsters. Sure, amongst the dust bunnies there were lost shoes, toy trucks, countless socks, the odd comic book, and a tape recorder, but no monsters. (When looking for monsters, you rarely notice tape recorders.) Mom left the light on, and I went back into my cold, haunted bed. I would have looked under my bed, but that required courage, and if I ever had it, I was all out. Beans or no beans, I pulled the covers over my head and shook with fear.

I was almost asleep when the unearthly sounds came back. Demonic, unholy reverberations emanating from directly beneath my bed—louder this time. The gates of hell opened up below my mattress. Very quickly, I determined my bed was an unsafe place to stay. I looked over at Dave, who was wearing the gorilla mask and staring right through me.

Adrenalin shot through my body, giving me the strength of 100 cowards. My soft covers were thrown off my bed and went crashing against the wall. I hovered over my mattress, kept aloft by the frantic flailing of my arms and legs. Shrieks don't accurately describe the sounds that came from my mouth, but dogs throughout the neighborhood howled in sync. I was as loud as any banshee. I ran from the room, leaving two sets of skid marks, one on the floor and the other conveniently hidden away from my sadistic brother's view inside my jammies.

Upon hearing my "scream of death," Mom and Dad came back into the room and confronted Dave. He was sitting in his bed, laughing hysterically at the prank he had pulled. He told them about the tape recorder and gorilla mask, and Mom and Dad really let him have it—they laughed and laughed and praised his creative genius. Then they turned toward me. I had crammed myself into the corner of the bedroom, defending myself from evil by brandishing the first means of defense I could lay my hands on, which happened to be a nerf ball. They comforted me by pointing and laughing.

That's my brother: Diabolical Dave. Mr. Sensitive.

Much later, in the morning after my medication had kicked in, I learned that we were to head up to Glacier for another bit of rest and relaxation. I was ecstatic up to the moment I learned that I would be sharing a tent with Dave. My sister Malady refused to share one with me. She was under the misimpression that sharing a tent with me would result in some sort of calamity befalling her, based on the grounds that the last time she shared a tent with me, she thought I had brought a skunk into it. That was blatantly false. I had never brought a skunk into the tent, I just led the skunk to the tent entrance, and the skunk, with no help from me, let himself in. But I couldn't point all that out to her, I just had to accept that I'd be sleeping with Dave, who, as a pimply, pubescent teen, would change his socks at regular monthly intervals and smelled only slightly better than Malady.

As usual, the family of twelve loaded up in the family station wagon: some kids in seats, some strapped to the luggage rack, and my little brother stuffed in the glove box. The six-hour trip to Glacier was uneventful, unless one counts teasing, punching, and pulling the car over as events. Along with punches, Dave regaled me with stories about the ferocious grizzlies that called Glacier home. He was expressing his other facet, fibber the know-it-all.

"You know, grizzlies might just be the most terribly vicious animals on the planet," he said. "Killers, they are. Horrible brutes. But they have cultivated a taste for little boys—you know, kids just about your size and shape"—he prodded me with a finger—"and texture." He went on to tell me every grisly detail about grizzly habits of feeding. How their claws were made to rip kid flesh and tear limbs right off the body's trunk. It was impossible to ignore him. He was telling me these awful stories, fibs even, but I was a willing audience. Some part of me wanted to hear these terrible tales.

As usual, upon the arrival of the Hagan family at Two Medicine, the tranquility and serenity of the valley was shattered. Tents were set up and sleeping bags laid out. As the kids went to gather firewood, Mom kindly warned us, "Watch out for bears."

With that warning, I started to think about the terrible tales Dave had told me. I didn't want to be alone, but the whole family fanned out, separating to get firewood. I was alone and stood still, listening. I could hear the others, not too far away, but I couldn't see them. I resolved to brace myself, show some courage, be brave. I took a single step, and a thunderous roar filled my ears. A loud, deep, bass bellow. Absolutely terrifying. I had flushed a grouse from its routine foraging. Not wanting to be the first human to be mauled by a bird and loaded with so much fear-generated adrenaline, I went back to camp at approximately the speed of light. Let the others gather wood.

Much later, after a dinner of the family favorite, weenie-o-bean, we gathered about the blazing campfire and charred marshmallows for s'mores. We toasted our marshmallows into hot lumps of carbon and mashed them between graham crackers and chocolate. Kids and s'mores just go together, and after eating a few s'mores, kids and pine needles, leaves, bird droppings, or whatever happens to be on the picnic table go together, too; we were a sticky mess.

My brother had so many dry, brown pine needles sticking to his marshmallowy hands, he looked like the wolf man, or just some teenager with really hairy palms (which, I suppose, should have gone unnoticed). I had brown pine needles stuck to my face, giving me the appearance of an eight year old whose DNA was blended with that of a porcupine. My sister was much better at not dropping her s'mores—no needles—but still very sticky. Mom took one look at us and ordered us to the restroom to clean ourselves up.

"Watch out for bears," she shouted as we left our site.

Washing up is pretty boring after a day of travel and camping chores, so along the way to the restroom I entertained myself by teasing my sister. "I'm not touching you," I said, pointing a pine-needle-encrusted index finger at her, "I'm not touching you." Along the way Dave, too, noticed that Mom's protective umbrella didn't quite work at this distance. WHAM! He started to pound that spot on my arm with his pine-needly fist. I was about to yell "Mom!" at the top of my lungs, but I

didn't. Something like rage welled up within me, and I hit him
back with my small golf-ball-sized fist, which I knew wouldn't
do much unless it was perfectly placed. I threw my tiny fist,
made contact, and ran as fast as my dinky little legs would
carry me. I headed for the woods with all speed, hoping to put
as much distance between me and my brother as possible. I
knew I would be in trouble once he caught me, but it would be
a while before his testicles dropped back into proper alignment.
I went deeper into the woods.

Obviously I didn't hit Dave as squarely as I had hoped; two
minutes later I heard him saying from the edge of the forest,
"Here, bear. Here, bear. C'mon, you grizzlies." Oh, brother, I
thought, can you believe that. ... He's trying to scare me with
... he ... Did he say BEAR?

Oops. Dang! How could I forget bears?! Every time I left
the camp, Mom said, "Watch for bears." Maybe I should go
back and make up with my brother. I'm sure he's all better
now and can see the error of his ways, picking on a small
child like me. I bet he's already thinking up a great apology
for hitting me in the arm. Bears! Oh, oh, I've got to get back
to camp. I bet Dave won't hit me.

"Here, bear ... Come on out, little brother, I've got some
knuckles with your name on 'em. ..."

Considering my options, I put my eight-year-old brain
through a crash course in logic. On the one hand, I could stay
in the woods, do a little exploring, and eat a few berries.
There probably wasn't a single bear within miles of here,
anyway. On the other hand, I could go out into the clearing
and face my brother.

"When I get my hands on you, you're gonna be one BIG BRUISE!"

"Stay in the woods it is," I thought to myself. When considering options logically, I gave bruises a prioritized ranking.

I'll just stay in the woods and start making my way back to camp, I reasoned. I followed what looked like a faint trail. On either side of the path were huckleberry bushes that were heavy with berries. I sampled a few, then a few more. There was a big bush just off the trail that had huge purple berries, so I went to it and picked until I saw another bush just a little farther off. Feeling confident, I tossed a few into the air and caught them on my tongue. A steady stream of purple hit my mouth (and occasionally my nose, eyes, and ears). I stayed in the woods eating berries, catching them in my mouth, but I failed to notice that the sun was now making a quick trip beyond the horizon and the colors surrounding me were beginning to lose their brilliance. I was eating what I considered to be the best food on Earth, even better than s'mores, and, at the time, that's all that mattered.

I came to a bush near a big fir tree and was plucking berries at a very low level when I had that "feeling." I suppose many of you have had that strange sensation when you know, *for a fact*, that someone is staring at you. You don't know how you know; you just know you are in someone's gaze: You are being observed closely. Everything in my body was telling me to move very slowly and look up.

There, just 18 inches away from me, were two tiny brown eyes just above a dirty blonde muzzle. A little black bear cub was partially hidden, both by the huckleberry bush and the fir tree. It was directly in front of me, and if I had wanted to,

I could have poked it in the eyes. But even as an eight year old, I figured eye-poking a bear could be a bad thing. Slowly, I drew myself up to my full height to show it how big I was. Apparently, 4 feet, 7 inches isn't enough to intimidate a bear, even a cub. With motion so slow only a time-lapse camera could detect it, I moved back a couple of paces. The bear never took his eyes off me, but he turned his head to the right just slightly, bent down and slowly grabbed a berry with his lower lip. Then he grabbed another and another, all the while keeping alert to my presence. While he was eating from the bush, I had a palm-full of berries in my left hand and was slowly placing them individually in my mouth with my right. There we were, just the two of us, for what could have been a lifetime, a little cub and I eating huckleberries.

I know now that where there is a cub, not far off is a mother with a grouchy disposition regarding threats to her offspring. But in my eight-year-old mind, I reasoned the little bear and I were now friends. Companions, buddies, who came together through fate and a patch of huckleberries. We just stared at each other, the cub and I, eating, each of us with a dark purple tongue. I was mesmerized by the bear in front of me.

The growl from behind caught me off guard. All my limbs froze. Even my blood froze, which was probably a good thing; anything less, and I would have had a major thaw under my belly button soaking my undies. I couldn't breathe or move as I listened to the crashing in the brush getting closer. Little bear heard the sound too and quickly dissolved mist-like into the brush. From behind, the growling was getting louder, and the snapping of branches indicated that it was coming fast! I was about to take a step in the same direction of the now vanished cub, when I was knocked violently to the forest floor. I had a great weight on my back. ... WHAM! WHAM! WHAM! Right in the arm!

Dave was laughing like a hyena on a sugar high. Shaking, I picked myself up and rubbed my arm where he hit me. Tears welled up in my eyes, and I stood there shocked. I wanted to tell him about the bear, but I wasn't at a point where I could speak, I was so stunned. Even if I could speak, something inside told me not to waste my breath on this jerk. I just stood there, waiting for my nerves to return.

"You should have seen yourself. Ha ha ha. You just froze like a statue. Did witto brudder wet his pants? Ha ha ha," Dave said. I peppered him with my remaining huckleberries and started to walk toward camp.

"Not that way," he said trying unsuccessfully to suppress his laughter. "C'mon, follow me. I'll get us back to camp." Wow, kindness, a new facet.

That night with all the family around the campfire, I told the story of the huckleberry cub. Especially highlighted was the part about how Dave ruined the whole once-in-a-lifetime experience. Because I was between Dave and the cub, he never saw the bear and said I made up the whole story. Shaking with rage, I called him a "dumbstupidmoronfreakfacedidiot-sonofabi" when Mom intervened and let it be known that it was now time for bed—no questions.

Reluctantly, we all got ready to hit the sack. We brushed our teeth, washed up, and got into our sleeping bags. We stayed up for a while telling horrible tales of bears and other critters.

"What if a bear was right outside the tent right now ... and there was a mountain lion too? Yeah, and a rabid wolverine ... and ..." And so it went into the night. Tales of terror in tents. Later, half asleep, I rolled over to see Dave holding a flashlight at his chin and wearing his gorilla mask. Funny; it didn't bother me at all. Come to think of it, it was a bit of an improvement.

A Very Short
Huckleberry Tale

S he said, "If you love me, do something special." So he set off in the morning light. He walked and walked until he came to meadow filled with wildflowers. They were of brilliant colors and smelled sweeter than any perfume. There, he picked and arranged the flowers and presented them to her.

"These are for you. I love you." he said.

"Flowers? What's so special about flowers? If you love me, do something special." So he set off with the hot afternoon sun beating down upon his shoulders. He walked and walked until he came to a meadow filled with huckleberries. They were ripe and purple and bursting with flavor. There, he picked and picked until he had a whole basket full. Then he presented them to her.

"These are for you. I love you." he said.

"Berries? What's so special about berries? If you love me, do something special." So he set off in a drizzling mist, into the evening. He walked and walked until he saw a dazzling rainbow over a mountain. He climbed the mountain and when he reached the top, he drew himself to his full height and grasped the rainbow. He held one end of the rainbow firmly and anchored it to the mountain. Then he threw the other end of the rainbow into the night sky, where it danced and made ribbons of light for all to see.

He returned and pointed up at the night sky and the northern lights and said, "These are for you. I love you." This time, she smiled at him and said, "Do you have any more of those berries?"

Getting Hired

Becoming a ranger in the National Park Service isn't easy. Not just anybody can go into a national park, waltz into the visitors' center, and demand a job. There are several rigorous screening procedures (including no waltzing) one must go through before getting hired. For example, all applicants must be a citizen of the United States or some other country and must have a valid birthday. Also, harsh as it may seem, all potential rangers are required to fill out an application. For many years, this stringent requirement kept me from becoming affiliated with the Park Service. But I eventually got a job. And the amazing thing is, I did it without filling out an application.

Ever since I was a little kid, I knew I wanted to live in Glacier. My family made several trips to that ice-sculpted land that left me hungry for more. But how could I find a way to live and hike up there? If I actually got a job, I might actually have to work. Work and I have never gotten along.

Maybe I could get a job whose main requirement was *walking away* from real work: hiking guides, for instance, don't actually work; they just stroll about with a smile on their face. I'd be good at that.

There are two types of employees hired by the Park Service: seasonal and permanent. The big difference between the two is that seasonal employees are employed for about three months, while permanent employees are year-round. In a huge park like Glacier, it can be hard to tell a seasonal from a permanent. Both types of employees have family, go to church, and play softball. We wear the same outfit and flat Smokey Bear hat (we take turns using it), so I thought I'd give you, the reader, a few handy hints to tell a seasonal from a permanent employee.

If you have ever passed through an entrance station, gone on a hike, listened to a campfire talk, seen a slide show program, asked a question at a visitors' center, had a ranger help you change a flat tire, or even gotten a speeding ticket, chances are you have seen a seasonal employee. On the other hand, if you have gone into a park and haven't seen anybody or talked to anyone, those are the permanent employees. They like to stay behind the scenes because they actually work.

Permanent employees of the Park Service are the cream of the government crop. Given the bad reputation of government workers all being slackers, let me tell you that the permanent employees I have seen give it their all, 110 percent of their effort, 110 percent of the time. They work extremely hard at a thankless job, they don't get any credit or accolades for their work, and they do it for less pay than many other government employees. Why do Park Service employees give so much and reap so little? It's simple: they're bad at math—on the pie chart of effort, you'll never see 110 percent.

Seasonals are very much like permanents in many respects: they work hard, but for a shorter period of time and for a lower wage, with no benefits. To distinguish between permanents and seasonals, just ask them a simple question: "Do you have health insurance?" A seasonal will always laugh at that one.

Everyone filling out a seasonal application is faced with a dilemma, for at the bottom of the application there are three blank spaces where the applicant must put in the names of their three preferred parks. Everyone I know *always* fills in Glacier first, and for the last two blank spaces, they *still* put in Glacier. These informed people know where they're going—the premier park in all the land. But some people who don't know better just arbitrarily fill in the other two blanks with some other inconsequential park like Yellows ... Yellowst ... Rotten Egg National Park, or some other silly place. Once the blanks are filled and the application is processed, the applicant is then put on a register and ranked. A list of the rankings is sent to a park, and the person doing the hiring starts at the top of the list and works her way down.

It could happen that two parks, for instance, Glacier and Rotten Egg, actually have the same applicant on their register. It could happen that Rotten Egg calls first and the applicant accepts. Then moments later, the personnel office of Glacier calls the very same applicant. Looks like the applicant has a decision to make. He's just been offered a job at *two* national parks and must choose one. Not too much of a dilemma, if you ask me. One offers pristine air, and the other keeps you asking, with a wrinkled nose, "Was that you?" Eventually, the smart applicant goes to Glacier. Those with no sense (of smell) go to Rotten Egg. But the point is, two parks can compete for one employee. That's what happened to me, not that two parks competed, but a dumb applicant had accepted a job at Glacier, *then* decided to go to Rotten Egg, freeing up the position at Glacier. It's a type of employment natural selection.

But seasonal or permanent, it's a heck of a job. Mountains, waterfalls, flowers, wolves, and grizzlies all right there in your office. The nearest wall is a glacial arête, and windows seem to open directly onto opportunity. But I had never considered actually applying for a job in Glacier—hell, that would take time and effort. Good thing that employee dropped off Glacier's roster.

Job-wise, I was pretty sure some random opportunity would come my way that summer—something always did. I just had to be patient. I had just put the tea pot on and was sitting at home, waiting for the phone to ring and the teapot to boil. My gaze shifted from the pot to the phone and back again. Pot to the phone. I was also working on a little Zen. I thought if I concentrated harder, I could make the pot boil faster. Eventually the phone rang, and I would have had it on the first ring, but it was held to the table by cobwebs.

"Hello," I said.

"This is Rod Ramsteel, with the National Park Service in Glacier," came the brusque voice from the other end. Not expecting a call from a ranger, I kept my conversation cordial.

"I had a fishing license ... and I released all those fish ... and I'm pretty sure I put that fire out. ..." I went to pour some tea, but I noticed the kettle was cold. I had forgotten to turn on the burner.

"I'd like to offer you a job as a naturalist with the National Park Service," came Rod's voice.

"But I never applied for a job. You sure you got the right number?"

"Yeah," he continued, "all the applicants on Glacier's roster list have taken jobs elsewhere. So I asked a few employees who are up here if they knew someone, *anyone* who wasn't working. Funny thing is, they *all* said you weren't; you've got quite a reputation. So do you want the job?"

Reputation indeed, I thought as I brushed away the cobwebs. I knew I wanted the job, but I didn't want to appear too eager. I wanted to show Ramsteel that I was a shrewd one who wouldn't take just any job.

"What are the benefits?"

"Huckleberries!" he said, not missing a beat.

"Are there any stock options?" I continued.

"Of course! Sometimes cattle get into the park, and we have to get them out. You can do it on foot or use a horse; so you've got a couple of options."

"Do you offer any health insurance?"

He stifled a snicker (I later found out he used to be seasonal). "Well, after a summer of hiking, you should be fit and trim, so yeah, I give you my *assurance* that you'll have toned calves."

I had heard enough. I knew I wanted to leave Anaconda and go somewhere I could actually do some work He sold me his benefits program. He really hooked me with the huckleberries.

"When can I start?" I asked.

"Yesterday would be nice. We're behind schedule, and I need you up here as soon as possible. I'm using what is called the Q Authority to hire you off the register; you'll be a 'lackey.'"

"Lackey?" I said.

"Yeah, a lackey. You, Pat, personally, *lack* the attributes that we really wanted in a new employee. But we'll take you on anyway. How soon can you get here?"

Mentally I calculated: from Anaconda to Glacier was about a six-hour trip. I needed to pack, not only clothing but food, camping gear, fishing tackle, and so on.

"I can be there in about five and a half hours," I said.

"Great, look forward to seeing ya," Ramsteel said, about to sign off.

"Hey," I chimed in, "who up there knew I wasn't working? Anybody I know?"

"Actually, there is a girl here you went to college with; her name is Beth."

"OK, yeah. I know Beth. I'll see you soon, Mr. Ramsteel."

As I hung up the phone and started to pack my stuff, I reminisced about the girl with whom I went to college, the one who recommended me for employment. I made a mental note that I'd have to thank her. I figured marrying her would express my gratitude. And, much later, that's just what I did. But that's another story.

So you see, the old cliché is true. It's not what you know that will get you a job. It's who you know.

Falling ... in Love

Is the glass half full or half empty? To many this old quandary is simply a matter of perspective. The volume of liquid in the glass really depends upon how we see things. For example, as we look at the contents of the glass, we must ask ourselves, "Is *this* glass mine?" (I always discreetly mark mine with a wad of chewing gum.) And if it is not your glass, what the heck does this type of question matter? Unless you realize, as you look at the glass, it is actually *your job* to fill it; for in life, sometimes our job is to pour for the drinkers, and therefore the glass is half empty. Still others say this adage helps explain how we view the world. Optimists are said to see the glass as half full. Beer drinkers firmly believe the glass is always half empty. Which is it? Speaking as an optimistic beer drinker, I know my glass should always be full, whether I'm drinking or pouring. Interestingly enough, this "half-and-half" poser also applies to the mountains within Glacier.

Many people say that Glacier National Park is filled with mountains. A multitude of steep, vertical, challenging, deadly, pointy peaks that must be scaled, scrambled, or otherwise climbed. Being afraid of heights, I've never really noticed the intimidating, lethal mountains. I prefer to keep a more level head or even look down while I hike, and I argue that Glacier is actually filled with spectacular valleys—hardly any mountains at all.

I guess I'm afraid of falling. Falling isn't good. When people fall, they get hurt—they get big old bruises, contusions, and boo-boos. There is no such thing as "good" falling, unless you're a lawyer. Lawyers see the world a little differently than moral people. The only thing they love more than the pull of gravity is the hard surface that immediately stops the fall and causes a boo-boo. They envision, through their legal-loophole eyes, people falling into large pools with wadded-up one hundred dollar bills cushioning the client's fall. But for the vast majority of normal, "responsible-for-your-own-actions" type of people, falling isn't good, unless you are falling in love. Lawyers don't like that kind of falling, unless there's a pre-nup in it for them.

Fear of falling from a very high place, or "heightophobia," is often confused with "acrophobia," which, when we break down the Latin, is actually fear of people in brightly colored spandex suits with sequins. For many people, fear of heights is normal, similar to the anxiety one feels regarding a tax audit or a visit to the proctologist. A social stigma is often applied to those suffering phobias, but being afraid doesn't make you a coward; rather, it just means you're a chicken.

The great irony is that my fear of falling aided my falling in love. If I weren't such a chicken, I don't think Beth would have ever noticed me. I don't exactly stand out in a crowd. I'm of average height, average build, and almost average intelligence. You've probably seen me a thousand times—but you overlooked me. For example, you know that guy at the football or baseball stadium who whips by on your TV screen when the camera goes as wide as it can and the faces in the crowd might as well be paper plates, but there is one guy who kind of stands out. You know the one: the guy wearing a baseball cap and frantically waving a big green foam hand and smiling. I'm happy to say, I'm the guy next to him—on the left. You've seen me, but I don't stand out.

Beth and I met in college. She made a huge impression on me but, to her, I was never more than an acquaintance. So I guess I'll start with the first time that I really made an impression on her: riding horses in the park.

One fine June day, Beth and I went riding horses to get to some cattle that had accidentally wandered into the park. Cattle do that. They wander into the park because sometimes the barbed wire is accidentally cut by people who accidentally see free grazing land. Anyway, Beth had gotten me the job with the Park Service, and I wanted to thank her by letting her take me riding with her. Beth was very familiar with horses. Back East, she was into what she called "riding English." She asked me if I rode "English." I didn't really understand her question but said English was the only language I wrote in.

We brought our heavy leather thingies from the tack shed—Beth called them saddles—to the corral fence. Then we called and whistled to the two horses. Beth had ridden these horses previously and was familiar with both. One was wild and kicking at the air, and the other was grazing contentedly on some grass. She went over to the calm one, patted it a few times and threw on the heavy leather thingy. She pulled and tugged some straps and then said, "Here you go. ... Serenity is all saddled up for you."

Now, at that point, I wanted to show Beth that I was a gentleman who believed in being chivalrous. It isn't quite accurate to say that I had a "crush" on Beth. It was much bigger than that; it was more like a "squash." Squashes, as we all know, are much bigger than crushes. And according to *Webster's Dictionary*, a "crush" is a case of "mild infatuation," whereas a "squash," according to Webster's, is "a plant in the member of the gourd family." From that, we can ascertain that *Webster's* is to be avoided when trying to define "love" (a tie, or equal score, in a tennis match). But a gallant gentleman doesn't leave a damsel to ride a wildly bucking horse while he rides a horse named Serenity. No, sir! I told Beth *she* would be riding Serenity.

I took my heavy leather thingy to the other horse, whose name was Fighting Bucker (apparently because he had a nasty habit of biting). I showed Beth real courage as I coaxed the animal to the fence, calmed it down, and placed the saddle on its back. I had never actually saddled a horse before, and I didn't really know what I was doing, but I didn't want to show my ignorance to Beth. I pulled on straps and thingies and whatnot. Shortly thereafter, Fighting Bucker was saddled, and he was under my total control. That horse knew I was boss. Like Beth, I, too, was an equestrian who could write English.

It was a short ride, but longer than I wanted. Apparently, you actually need to pull and secure the straps and leather thingies. Beth was way ahead of me, and I wanted to catch up to her, so I dug my heel into Fighting Bucker's ribs. On normal horses, that works like an accelerator on a car, but Fighting Bucker apparently had some brain disorder, and it caused him to jump and spin wildly. I held on, but my saddle was a little too loose and worked its way to the underside of the horse.

Luckily, my butt was several feet above the horse when the saddle went to his underside. Upon landing back on Fighting Bucker, I wisely dropped the reins and threw my arms around the horse's neck. I was still slipping off to the side, so, in order to maintain my position on the top side of the horse, I sunk my teeth into the horse's neck. He showed his displeasure by accelerating to something just under light speed. I tried to calm him by talking in a soothing tone, but horses just don't understand English too well, especially when you are speaking with a mouthful of their flesh. "MMMmmphrrrraaaagh," I said in what I thought was a clear manner.

We were closing in on Beth, and I held on for dear life—but dear life was slowly slipping away. All the jarring and bumping caused me to slide off the top side of the neck, to the underside, giving me a good look at Fighting Bucker's lower jaw. It was at that point, galloping along with the saddle hanging from the belly and me hanging onto the underside of the horse's neck, that we passed Beth and Serenity, who were moving at a comfortable "mosey." To show Beth I was still in control, as we passed, I casually remarked "Yee HAHHHH-HHHHHHHHHHHH."

The water of Paradise Creek finally peeled me off the lower side of the horse's neck. The ford was plenty deep, and miraculously, I didn't get bashed upon rocks or trampled by Fighting Bucker's hooves. I stood in the middle of the creek, feeling for broken bones, which was difficult with loads of Fighting Bucker's mane in each hand. I would have dropped the hair, but at the time my hands were still in "dear life" mode and wouldn't yet open. Beth climbed off her horse and smiled. Fighting Bucker slowly came over to me in the middle of the creek, as if to say, "Hay!" (horses often misspell that one) "You're alright for a human." Then, knowing turnabout is fair play, he bit me in the neck.

It was just after that episode that Beth started to refer to me as Pat, instead of the usual, "hey you" or "that guy." She *noticed* me but kept her distance (I learned later that it was for my own protection).

Later in June, a friend of mine, Paul Hillary, came over to my Park Service hut while I was working on the plumbing. Paul, a distant relative of some guy named Sir Edmund Hillary, knew I hated "work" and offered to help. My reputation regarding physical labor is known parkwide. Paul had been told that I was orphaned in the wilderness and raised by a pack of sloths. Alone, I would have had that pit dug in the blink of an eye, but then again, I perform physical labor within a geological time frame. Paul decided to help speed things up. The plumbing of a hovel doesn't take too much skill, just a spade, and we dug the pit together; Paul from within the pit and me lying in the sun in my Park Service thong and shades, all slathered in oil. When we were done, we pushed the out-house over the hole and then went to my hovel. I went to the fridge and poured two glasses of beer; lying in that sun had made me hot. Paul was mildly thirsty too. While we let the drinks cool us off, we discussed life and our plans.

"Think I'm gonna climb Mount Wilbur tomorrow. You want to come?"

Despite its wimpy, Mr. Ed-ish name, Mount Wilbur is one of the more intimidating peaks in the park. I listened intently, then said, "I think that's my glass—you've got the wrong beer mug."

"Oh, okay, here," he said, handing me the loaded mug. "So, you want to climb Wilbur?—Hey, this other mug is empty." True, so I politely refilled his glass.

"As I was saying, I'm gonna climb ... Ugh! ... There's a wad of gum on this mug."

"Oops, that's right; that *is* my mug." I smiled, and we exchanged mugs. "You still haven't answered my. ... Hey! You just gave me an empty mug!" He grabbed the bottle for himself. He had some trouble asking me to climb. I guess he was nervous or distracted, but finally we decided to climb Wilbur.

Initially, I suggested that we climb the prairie meadows of Two Dog Flats, but Paul would have none of it. I wouldn't mind falling off Two Dog Flats; falling there would require a running start and a rock to trip me (but I'd see it a mile away). I would most certainly plunge at least my full body height into a cushy, leafy, pillow-soft clump of balsam root, or possibly I'd trip and fall into St. Mary's Lake. Both of which I could handle. Paul said Two Dog Flats wasn't even a hike, let alone a climb, and that he wanted to climb Wilbur, a fall off of which would last approximately seven minutes. Seven minutes of hysterical, panic-filled screaming and clawing at the air. Then, you'd plunge into the icy waters of Iceberg Lake ... that is, if you didn't smack an iceberg; which I guess would probably be a good thing to put out the fire caused by reentry. No, I would have none of it, but then Paul said, "Beth is going."

"What time are we leaving?" I asked.

Early the next morning, Paul and Beth came to the hovel. They both looked fresh, invigorated, and ready for the climb. I, however, was in a much sorrier state. I hadn't slept a wink. I had nightmares in which I saw my body bouncing down a cliff and splatting onto an iceberg. Starting at about 5:00 a.m., I had been doing nothing but nervously staring at a wall and chugging coffee.

We loaded into Paul's car and headed to Wilbur. Along the way, I wanted to portray myself as a suave and sophisticated man, a man of derring-do that women fawn over—kind of like Sean Connery, but without the muscle or the eyebrows or much else. I said to Beth, "Rowllblurberrr," or rather, that's what my lower intestine said. (When I drink too much coffee, my innards get a little chatty, especially around cute women.) In a small car in the early morning hours, my colon proved to be quite a conversationalist—one who lectured at length and didn't approve of interruption. It was about a thirty-minute lecture.

As we pulled into the parking lot, Wilbur loomed ominously. Though it was a clear day, sunny and warm with birds flitting about, I pictured lightning and dark black clouds enfolding Wilbur (there was also scary music, as in *Jaws*, but I seemed to be the only one who could hear it).

"What a beautiful day!" Beth exclaimed.

"Do you hear that?" Paul said dramatically, cupping a hand to his ear.

"I can't help it—it's the damned coffee," I snapped.

"No," Paul said, "the mountain; it has a message for us. It says, 'Climb me.'"

I got a different message; similar to one in the movie *Field of Dreams*, in which the owner of the field keeps hearing the whispered words, "If you build it, they will come." I looked at Wilbur and on that day heard the words, "If you fall, it will hurt." I wanted out.

"I gotta go to the bathroom," I said and sprinted toward the toilet in the campground, leaving Paul and Beth to unload the day packs.

Inside the outhouse, I told myself to get a grip, show some courage, and be brave. My mantra, one I've had since pre-school, was "I think I can. I think I can. I think I can." I repeated my mantra in a loud, clear voice, over and over, to bolster my courage. In the solitude of the wooden outhouse, I felt my resolve come together, gel, and solidify with each "I think I can." Coming out of the outhouse, I expected to meet Beth and Paul back in the parking lot, but no, there they were, right there.

"Uh," Paul said cautiously, "you still up for going?"

"Yeah," I said, "I think I can ... climb it."

"You sure?" said Beth.

"Yeah, I think I can."

The climb was easy, at least the lower grassy parts. But then came the steep, rocky section, with pointy bits. Paul and Beth scrambled easily upward. I took a more cautious approach and climbed using my hands, feet, teeth, nails, earlobes, and other body parts. It was slow, but using "head jams" instead of the usual "finger jams" in the cracks of the rock seemed prudent. There was one part near the top, a hole in the rock I believe is called "Thin Man's Pleasure," where I experimented with a technique called the "whole body jam." Thin Man's Pleasure is like a donut ring of rock where the climber has to go through the hole. People like Paul, Beth, and those suffering from anorexia go right through the hole of the donut. I'm not fat, but there are places on my body that have "extra fluffy skin," and I plugged the hole. I was stuck in Thin Man's Pleasure. My arms extended inward, toward the mountain, while my legs dangled and kicked in space. Having already passed through, Beth took one arm and Paul the other, and they tugged in unison. No luck, but then Paul pulled some suntan oil from his pack and greased me up. I came out with an audible pop, like a champagne cork. The worst was behind us. Finally, after hours of effort, we made it to the top.

Much to my surprise, the weather was nice on top. Paul and Beth enjoyed the views by walking right up to the edge and looking straight down into Iceberg Lake. I gathered my courage and took baby steps toward the edge. I leaned out, looked at the baby blue waters flecked with brilliant white chunks of ice, and gave a squeal—not of delight, either. Beth and Paul looked at me strangely, silently.

My normal response to such looks—"I'm out of beer?"—didn't work. Paul looked down and shook his head. But Beth smiled.

Going back down, we stopped at Thick Man's Plug (as it truly should be called). I couldn't climb down it—it was just too steep—so Paul put a harness on me so both he and Beth could rappel me down. I was roped up and lowered over the edge of the plug. I couldn't help it: I looked between my legs and screamed in horror. Pointy, rocky spikes were below me. All my worst dreams were coming to pass. Paul was telling me to calm down, and Beth offered encouragement. They didn't seem to realize that my life was held by a thin rope, probably manufactured in Tahiti where falling isn't an issue, and I was dangling off into nothingness, into space, with hard pointy things below.

I screamed for what seemed a lifetime. It took them seven minutes to lower me to safety. Seven minutes of hysterical, panic-filled screaming and me thrashing wildly and clawing at the air. When my feet eventually made contact with terra firma, I took the rope out of the harness and French-kissed the ground. I think it kissed me back too—and it was good.

The rest of the descent was an easy walk. As we walked back to the car, I could tell Wilbur, the ominous mountain, had taken its toll on Paul, because he now had a mantra of his own: "Never again, Never again." Beth seemed as energetic as ever. She glowed from a combination of the day's work and the sun. We chatted a little on our way to the car.

"The horse, the mountain—I think you like to scream and fall—or something. It's always an adventure with you." She smiled.

Mountain Men Don't Wear Pants

Ever since I was a young boy, I have had a dream. A dream wherein I'm standing in the Amazon jungle in my "Oscar the Grouch" underwear, surrounded by blonde bikini-clad Amazon warriors. But for obvious reasons, that isn't the dream I'm going to talk about. Another dream I have long had is that of being a mountain man. A rugged, bearded man who has left the creature comforts of society behind. A man who willingly exposes himself to nature's extremes—bitter cold, pouring rain, raging fire—a man clad in fringed buckskin who lives the life of a hermit, alone in the wilderness; a man challenging the elements as well as himself.

When I was in fourth grade, I wanted to be just like Jeremiah "Liver Eatin'" Johnson, or at least like Robert Redford (though maybe taller). I thought the girls in my school would just love to have a mountain man seated next to them, and I

once asked a sweet girl, Rosie Carbuncle, to accompany me
on a foray out into the wilderness of my backyard. I showed
her how mountain men would live off the land by eating edible
plants. I showed her how to eat aspen leaves by the handful
and, later, how to vomit aspen leaves, just like a real mountain
man. Mountain men, I later realized, were much smarter than
your average ten year old trying to impress a girl.

The dream of being a mountain man didn't fade much over
the years. It has always been with me. I think it has stayed with
me for two reasons: I live in Montana, a state with enough
wilderness to make this dream come true, and I love to play
with the tools of the mountain-man trade; namely, matches
and hatchets. But I am a realist and understand there are some
drawbacks to a life of isolation. Number one: I can't be a true
hermit; my wife (yeah ... Beth married me) and family won't
let me. Number two: The outdoors can be kinda scary. Yet
somehow the dream persists. It crawls on its belly, under a hail
of arrows, into my psyche.

Years ago, when my daughter Emma was three, I was just
lounging around the house in my boxers, as I am wont to do.
My wife doesn't want that particular wont. She doesn't think
it dignified to lounge about the house in your underwear. I
explained that the boxers look just like Bermuda shorts, with
the added benefit of immediate access for scratching, but to
no avail. Women just don't understand men and the special
relationship they have with their underwear.

As my wife and I were discussing underwear standards, the
phone rang. Because she was beginning to get the upper hand in
the argument, I crossed the room to pick it up, thus cutting her

off and therefore winning the dispute. On the line was Scott Emerson, a ranger from Glacier National Park, who asked if we'd like to volunteer our services in a remote part of the park. He explained that we would be isolated, an hour from the nearest town (population: 12), and living in a turn-of-the-century log cabin. As he continued to list the details of the job, I got lost in my own thoughts. My mind strayed from the conversation, and, just like on television, a dream sequence started. I was picturing myself as a mountain man, "Aspen Eatin' Hagan," growing a beard, wearing a coonskin cap, and squinting into a spectacular sunset, one calloused hand wrapped around my trusty rifle, the fingers of the other hand playing with a bear-claw necklace. Then the dream sequence abruptly ended, and I was brought back to reality by the voice of the ranger.

"Well? Will you take the position?"

"Yes, of course," I replied, in a deep mountain-man voice (not unlike Clint Eastwood).

"Are you okay?" asked Scott. "Your voice sounds a little funny. Are you sick? 'Cause I can get someone else. ..."

"No!" I screeched, my gruff voice cracking back into its normal pre-pubescent range (not unlike Peter Brady). "We'll take it," and I hung up the phone before he could change his mind.

I smiled at my wife. She stood across the room, her arms akimbo. I couldn't wait to share the news. "Honey! Pack your bags! We just landed a job in the wilderness where we get to live in a log cabin!" I watched her face closely. She didn't look quite as excited as I had hoped. I think she was picturing me throwing hatchets in my undies.

"We need to talk," she said calmly.

"No time!" I said. "Gotta pack! Gotta go!"

With the benefit of hindsight, I wish I would have sat down and talked with her. That, at least, would have calmed me down enough to think clearly while I was frantically packing. Hours later, we were on the road; I was quite excited, but I couldn't shake the feeling that, in my haste, I had forgotten to pack something.

The trip to Glacier National Park was a long, hot one. It was about six hours of driving in our little Yugo Lemoan, a car that fit nicely into our volunteer budget but didn't have any frilly amenities like air conditioning. Beth rolled down her window, and I stripped to the waist and rolled mine down. As I did so, I realized I was still in my underwear, but Beth kept silent on the issue, apparently because I wasn't constantly scratching. As the mountains drew ever closer, I realized that I was on the cusp of a dream. This would be my chance to transform my mild-mannered self into a hardened mountain man.

We pulled into the ranger station to pick up the key for our cabin. A ranger I assumed to be Scott Emerson was on the porch, cleaning a gun, as we came to a stop. I hopped out of the car and realized, as my feet hit the ground, that I had been sitting for an awfully long time and my legs were tingly asleep and wouldn't properly support me. I staggered over toward my new boss. Immediately Scott stood up, knocking over the chair he'd been sitting in, and leveled the gun with a worried look in his eye.

"Whoa! Stop right there, you nutcase—take another step and I'll ..."

I looked behind me for the "nutcase" but I didn't see one. Then it hit me. I completely understood. I knew who the nutcase was, and at precisely the same moment, I realized what it was that I had forgotten to pack; a pair of pants.

Emerson, being a reasonable man, lowered his weapon from his shoulder, but appeared to be ready to shoot from the hip if need be. I explained to him that I was his new volunteer for Kintla Lake and that I needed the key to open the cabin. The look he gave me was one of a man in torment. A man who refused to believe what he saw. Keeping his gun level, he backed into the ranger station. Outside, I could hear a drawer open and the jangle of keys. He came outside, still with the gun leveled, but with a set of keys to boot. When he was closer he threw the keys to me. I couldn't help but notice how quickly his hand returned to the gun after tossing me the keys. He pointed in the direction of our duty station with the barrel. Feeling a bit awkward, I left.

I'm sure later, when Emerson calmed down, he would tell his fellow rangers about the perils of hiring someone over the phone. He'd tell them why it might be important to *see* an applicant prior to hiring. Because one time, he hired a guy who by all appearances drank too much and wore nothing– nothing–but his underwear.

Another hour on the road, and we reached the lake where our cabin stood. The cabin was perfectly suited for my mountain-man endeavor. Situated at the foot of the lake, with mountains jutting 5,000 feet above the water's surface, it was a cute one-room cabin, a little small, but cozy. It didn't have any electricity, but if I gave Emma a bucket and sent her to the stream, it would have running water.

We hauled our luggage a quarter of a mile or so from our car to the cabin and began to settle in. Emma carried the lighter bags, Beth carried the heavier, and I carried on with my fantasy of being a mountain man. I would face a new challenge. I knew I had made a bad impression on my boss, arriving in my underwear, but in the future I could avoid further embarrassment simply by steering clear of him. I was stuck in an awkward situation because I had forgotten to pack any pants. Maybe pants are more socially acceptable, but mountain men aren't encumbered by social norms. They do things their way—and sometimes that means no pants at all.

I recalled the incredible story of John Colter, one of the most famous of all mountain men. Colter was captured and stripped naked by the Blackfeet and then sent running across the countryside looking for a men's clothier. Deer and antelope would interrupt their play to snicker at the "streaker of the plains." But Colter was a true mountain man. He covered 200 miles of harsh terrain barefoot and without a stitch of clothing. He endured bitter temperatures and the jeers of wildlife. If he could survive without pants, so could I. With courage undaunted, I went forward in my mountain man quest.

Turning my thoughts back to the situation at hand, I took inventory of the resources that the cabin held. Though I have no background in interior decoration, one could accurately describe the cabin's motif as "early Spartan." It held a bed, a table, and for the recreational pyromaniac, a wood stove. Illumination was provided à la Coleman.

I stared in fascination at the stove and the lanterns. As a certified recreational pyromaniac and fledgling mountain man, I thought it essential that they should be ignited as soon as possible—even midday. Enthusiastically, I groped around in my pants pockets searching for some matches. Then I remembered that I wasn't wearing pants.

"Honey," I said, "got any matches?" I don't know why she was so reluctant, but after a short pleading period of twenty minutes, I wore her down and got the matches. As I was leaving the cabin, Beth said, "Please be careful." Emma heard this too and said, "Yeah, Daddy, don't get hurt again."

"Don't worry," I said, "we mountain men are always careful. Hand me that lantern, would you?" I left the cabin.

I came back with the lantern glowing. But due to some manufacturing defect, this particular lantern seemed to generate more heat than light, so I would have to carry it with one hand and then quickly change hands.

"Honey!" I shouted, "I got it lit!"

"That's nice," she said inspecting my handiwork, "but the fire is supposed to be on *the inside* of the lantern. Now take it outside before you burn the cabin down."

As I turned to go, Emma whispered to Beth, "Daddy lost his eyebrows, didn't he?"

Most mountain men are men of action and not words, so I didn't comment. I knew perfectly well my eyebrows weren't lost. They were on the porch, smoldering, right next to my bangs, right where I left them. Lost indeed …

If I was going to be a mountain man, I knew my hands would need a callous, at least one. So next on my agenda was wood chopping, axe wielding, and/or hatchet throwing. I thought these activities would be much safer since they didn't involve any facial hair, and we needed some kindling for our wood stove. My wife was quick to point out that there was a whole cord of stacked, dried kindling; ready to use. She just didn't understand my quest.

The hatchet provided by the Park Service was as sharp as a surgeon's scalpel. I went to the wood pile (unchopped stuff), selected a hefty piece of lodgepole pine, and sauntered over to the chopping block. I held the wood firmly in my left hand and my trusty hatchet in my right. Quickly, in mountain-man fashion, I forcefully brought the hatchet down. Suddenly, a white light filled my eyes. The pain was incredible. I couldn't hold back—I screamed.

My wife rushed out of the cabin, only to see me clutching my hand between my thighs and writhing on the ground.

"Pat! Stop yelling and let me see your hand!" I offered my hand for inspection. Emma, who oddly enough is always prepared for these types of situations, came out of the cabin with her Sesame Street Doctor's Kit firmly in hand.

"Emma," my wife said gently, "come here and open your bag." From the bag my wife drew forth the red plastic tweezers. Beth explained to the young one, "Momma has to pull a sliver from Daddy's hand." My wife pulled on the giant sliver, and I screamed in pain with each tug. Emma found a stout stick and placed it in my mouth, explaining simply, "Bite, Daddy." I bit down, and my wife tugged again. I felt the wood coming out, but the pain was too intense. My world dissolved and went black.

As I was coming to, my wife was showing Emma the enormous sliver. "See, there it is—right there." Even in my delirium, I could tell she was proud of me because she was saying something about "... some mountain man."

Dare to dream, and with luck, you too can be a mountain man. A man like John Colter or "Liver Eatin'" Johnson. But there will only be room in the wilderness for one "Aspen Pukin' Hagan."

Oh, Yummy!
Brussels Sprouts!

It was one of those nights. Beth and I were burrowed deep under the warm quilt. I looked over at my sleeping wife's face. She was still aglow, and a faint smile played upon her lips. I rolled over, feeling exhausted and satisfied. I looked up at the twinkling stars and thought, "We really need to fix the roof of this cabin." The old cabin could use some tender, loving care, but it could wait. It just didn't seem important right now. Right now was a quiet, magical time, a time to bask in each other's warmth. Beth and I were both content, satisfied, and spent. And deservedly so; we had gotten Emma, our three-year-old daughter, to eat her vegetables.

I know some people think there are greater problems out there than getting your kid to eat veggies. They have a valid point. Parents should be more worried about their children getting into nasty drugs than whether their kid eats broccoli or not. But my kid was three years old. The only drug I worried about her getting into was Drano or something else with a childproof lid. Of course, a three year old can be quite impressionable, and scaring them away from drugs is relatively easy. Just show them a picture of Keith Richards–works every time. But veggies are another matter.

The problem of kids and vegetables is nothing new. For thousands of years, eating vegetables has caused domestic wars waged across tabletops: parents versus children. In the early days, cavemen had a peaceful existence; they never argued across the table because they ate meat and had no tables. But historically, we know that even the ancient Greeks were vexed by vegetables. The great philosopher, Play-Doh, tackled this issue head on. At his house, little toga-clad kids were playing with a substance that would later bear his name, when they were all called together at the table to share a meal of mashed turnips. The urchins whined and refused to eat. The great philosopher quickly went to work. After considerable thought, which is what he did professionally, he is known to have given the small ones some very sage advice: "Quit your whining, and eat your vegetables." Parents all over the world were quick to pick up on this philosophical tidbit and have been quoting Play-Doh from across the table for generations.

My dad was something of a student of Play-Doh. Frequently, he would quote the master's teachings while simultaneously testing his personal decibel range. But my mother was a little more progressive; she liked to use good old-fashioned Catholic guilt.

"You really should eat those beets. Don't you know kids across the globe would be happy to have a plate with so much food? Kids are starving in India."

"Name one," I replied.

Mom, I would later realize, was also a student of Play-Doh. But I digress. Beth, Emma, and I had left our tiny, dilapidated trailer in East Glacier and moved up into a wild, remote part of the park known as the Northfork. We were stationed at Kintla Lake, where we occupied a nice log cabin built in the early Pleistocene. The chinking was coming out from between the logs; some planks on the front porch needed replacing; and there were a couple of hula-hoop-sized holes in the roof, which conveniently let the bats out. We were very comfortable. The home provided by the Park Service was exactly like our real home.

Kintla Lake is a long way from everywhere. The nearest grocery store was about three and a half hours away, traveling a bumpy, dusty, dirt road. Additional time had to be added for meeting oncoming vehicles. The road in many places was too narrow to accommodate two cars passing, so one would have to back up until space was found to let the other car pass. You can't miss a Northfork local when they come into town; they're the ones with the side-view mirrors dangling on their doors and small fir trees hanging from their bumpers. Getting groceries could be quite a time-consuming adventure, so we limited ourselves to a trip to town once every three weeks.

At the cabin we had been living what anthropologists call a "can-to-mouth" existence. Our meals consisted of opening a can and warming it on the wood stove. Day after day, can after can, eating became a function of subsistence rather than gustatory delight. There is only so much happiness cans of beef stew and cans of peas or carrots can bring into your home. But you might be surprised at how much discord they can bring.

Typically, at dinnertime, we would put Emma into her chair, which attaches directly to the thick wooden table. The kid's chair is a holdover from the Spanish Inquisition and is designed to keep three-year-old infidels from going anywhere until the parental grand inquisitors are satisfied the little one has cleaned her plate. If the parents are satisfied, the kid can get down. The chair is pure genius as far as I'm concerned. Once the tyke is secure, we then present a masterpiece meal of beef stew with carrots or, to break the monotony, peas and beef stew.

The stage is set. All the plates and participants are in place for the evening's drama. Mom, Dad, and chair-bound tot.

We all dive in and work on the food. I try to be a good example and get it over with quickly. Beth gently places her hand over mine, because my utensils are throwing sparks, and I, too, slow to a more genteel pace. Three-year-old Emma will eat her stew, if somewhat reluctantly, but then comes to the corner of her plate with the vegetables and the inevitable impasse. Emma sits, wearing a bright red bib that, upon closer inspection, turns out to be her lower lip. The big lower lip look works on most parents, but not us. My wife and I have chosen our sides, and we are on the side of the vegetables. Emma toys a bit with some carrots, pushing them but not consuming them. Beth and I then go to work.

"Hey, Emma! If you eat your carrots, you'll grow big and strong!" Beth said.

Emma just crossed her arms and turned her head up and away from her plate. She turned her head far enough to give Linda Blair a shock.

"Hey, Emma!" I spoke up. "If you eat your carrots, you'll have good eyes and be able to see in the dark!"

No response.

Beth tried again. "Emma, did you know that carrots are high in vitamins? They are soooo good for you. Hey, Bugs Bunny loves carrots!"

Emma said nothing–but stuck her lip out further, so that a fold rests on her lap. "Hey, Emma!" I said, changing my tone. "If you eat carrots, you won't die in your sleep tonight!"

With the benefit of hindsight, I now know *that* one was probably not used by Play-Doh. My wife is a student of philosophy, and she let me know, in no uncertain terms, that one wasn't to be used again. We had to come up with a better plan to get our kid to eat veggies. We would start by eliminating the can.

Since we were so far away from a grocery store, we thought it would be fun (not to mention practical) to augment our diet with edible plants found in the area. Wild plants are an often overlooked source of food simply because they might be poisonous or taste like old hobo shoes. But by grabbing a book and educating yourself, you can avoid the poisonous ones and just eat the ones that taste like old hobo shoes. It's amazing what the outdoors can do to your appetite. On our next trip into town, we got a book on edible plants and some fresh brussels sprouts.

From the book *Grubs and Other Natural Foods: Foraging to a Thinner You*, we learned about the edible native plant species.

The book has numerous tasty recipes for wild plants like serviceberry, huckleberry, fireweed, glacier lilies, tree bark, and pond scum.

Wild plants enabled us to stretch our meager volunteer budget, and we felt that we were living closer to the land. But one drawback is that many of these plants are seasonal. You can't eat fireweed in the early fall (actually, you can, but its taste is like a blend of a two-by-four and an all-season radial with just a dash of hobo shoe) or huckleberries in the spring. But according to our book, there is a wild green that we can gather any time of year—spring, summer, fall, or winter: lichens.

Now, maybe it is a stretch to call lichens a "wild green" since they come in a broad spectrum of colors: red, black, orange, and paisley. There are lichens on rocks that mountain goats eat that really stick to the rock, forcing the goats to use special tools (chisels) to remove them. There are lichens that look like fall leaves: brown or green and all wrinkled. But the lichen the book told us to gather was a black-tree lichen, most commonly called "Old Man's Beard" but sometimes referred to as "French Pits."

This hair-like lichen grows from tree branches in most forests in Montana and is a protein-rich winter food source for deer, moose, elk, and desperate people three to four hours away from grocery stores. After gathering about one or two armfuls of the lichen, we brought it back to the kitchen, opened our cookbook to a page with a big fat grub on it, and decided we weren't that hungry after all. After a lengthy pause, we reopened the book to the correct page and looked under the appetizing heading, "Lichen: Black Gelatinous Mass."

To prepare this culinary delight, all you have to do is add your lichen to a pot of boiling water. Though the book doesn't call for it, I would recommend having a bottle of catsup, mustard, mayonnaise, hot sauce, or even latex paint at the ready to cover up the taste. According to the book, you simply boil the lichens until you have "a black gelatinous mass" (hence, the catchy name) and then add catsup to taste and for some wild contrast in color. Though it isn't in the book, for a festive little dessert with this dish, I recommend brussels sprouts.

Well, now we were ready to get our little Emma to eat vegetables without a fuss. Beth and I put on our game faces.

My little daughter's face just lit up upon the presentation of this dish. She stared silently at the plate for about one minute, which is a long time for a three year old to sit and silently stare at anything, let alone a plate. Emma looked at me, then back at her plate. As if to confirm her worst fears, she asked, "Dinner?"

Beth and I glued on our masks of insincerity. We smiled all the time and spoke as though we were overdosed on Prozac.

"Yes, Emma!" I said. "Doesn't this dinner look fun?! It's like pudding, but with hair! And guess what we are having for dessert!"

"Dad, you're scaring me—you're using a lot of exclamation points."

"Yes, you perceptive child! Tonight, we'll be having brussels sprouts for dessert! You like dessert ... don't you?" I said in my best Mr. Rogers voice.

Emma's eyes fell upon the plate. Searching for help, she looked over at my wife, her loving mother.

"Mom," she said in a weak, trembling voice, "do we really ... have to eat this?" My wife stared at her own plate containing the black mass and visibly shivered. The black gelatinous mass shivered too.

Trembling, looking pale, and suppressing a gag, my wife said with tears welling in her eyes, "It's ... good for ... (gag) ... you, honey. Deer like it!"

Emma took her spoon and dipped it into the black gelatinous mass that looked like pudding experiencing both a bad attitude and a bad hair day. She twirled the spoon. Little bits of lichen clung to the utensil, resembling a hairball spit up by a cat. Between gags, Beth and I continued to eat. Emma pulled the spoon out of the dark pile and watched a blob fall back onto the plate with an audible plop. She sighed heavily and then, afraid to use her slimy spoon, reached over and plucked a brussels sprout off her plate and popped it into her mouth. Then she grabbed another. Oh, yes, we were satisfied.

Well, she ate her vegetables. Wasn't that simple?

It's amazing how life in the boonies has helped our family grow and develop. It's like that old cliché: "Where there's a will, there's a dead guy." He probably died eating lichen. We went to Kintla Lake with nothing, but we left with nothing, too. We depleted our stock of canned goods and felt confident we could now eat anything, including French cuisine consisting of snails. Emma certainly grew, physically and emotionally. Back at our house she eats everything; she is no longer intimidated by a plate of fresh "greens." She fears nothing. Well, that's not exactly true. She is deathly afraid of Keith Richards.

Uniformity

They say that women "love a man in uniform." Women are silly that way. There is nothing attractive or sexy about a man in uniform. I've seen men in uniforms, and they do nothing for me. Uniforms are boring, especially with men in them; women in them aren't much better. Men, however, like women in a silky negligee. That truly works for me. I know it's a double standard, but it's one I can live with. If it were a just and equitable world, men would wear negligees too. Thank goodness it isn't an equitable world. Can you imagine a meeting in the war room of the Joint Chiefs of Staff in which the president is surrounded by his top military advisers, and they are all wearing that little lacy "something special" from Frederick's of Hollywood? Negligees and hairy backs. That's just wrong. Some double standards are okay. Uniforms will have to do.

Many government employees have very practical, snappy-looking uniforms. Take the navy, for example. While onboard ship, sailors wear those white suits with blue bandana–type necks and floppy white hats. This ensemble looks very nice, and as a whole, the uniforms are very practical in the sense that they are excellent for getting wet. And I'm pretty sure the navy's white cloth hat was the inspiration for the plastic dog dish. I've suggested to the navy that they move the blue bandana to the front of the uniform. There it could act as a bib and save the taxpayers thousands of dollars in paper napkins. Of all the services, Marines have the best uniforms. They get swords. Never, ever, make fun of people in snappy uniforms with swords. Marines are good people.

In the Park Service, we are not very snappy dressers. We wear dull, lifeless, earth tones: green and gray. Walls in many Park Service buildings are painted so as to hide employees from the visiting public. Outdoors you can't see them either. Green and gray blend right into the woodwork. How are you supposed to find camouflaged employees? Park Service uniforms should be vibrant and alive. Bright orange, like modern prison uniforms. Now that stands out. But, alas, for now we're stuck with green and gray. No one should have to view such a fashion faux pas. Look around you right now. I'll bet no one is wearing that color combo of green and gray. People don't wear those colors by choice. They wear them because it's their uniform and their bosses make them.

I've decided to take an in-depth look at the history of Park Service clothing. It is well known that seasonal employees have too much time on their hands in the winter, so I've decided that I will not let my hands become the devil's play-things. I'm going to delve into made-up fashion history. It's either that or do real work—so fake fashion history it is.

It started on the fashion runways of long ago. President Ulysses S. Grant established the nation's first national park, Yellowstone, in 1872. He quickly followed up, in true executive style, by immediately establishing the Park Service forty-four years later, in 1916. Historians will note that Grant could do this so quickly because he was no longer encumbered with any job. (Historians will also note that Grant died in 1885, but what do they know about fashion, anyway? Have you seen the way historians dress?) Male models would parade up and down the runway, wearing various potential Park Service togs, strike a dramatic pose, then turn and get a real job in an off-Broadway musical production.

In any case, the new Park Service needed to be outfitted, and so uniform selection proceedings began. It was decided that the uniform's color scheme would be one that evoked a significant response from the public. Primary-colored paisley and feather boas got no reaction at all. However, when the public got its first look at the green and gray, they responded unanimously with an immediate yawn.

Initially, Park Service clothes were both functional and fashionable. In the olden days, rangers used to wear big old baggy pants called "jodhpurs." For the uninitiated, jodhpurs are pants with great big bulging sides, such as seen on Dudley Do-Right. Rangers would roam the great outdoors wearing their jodhpurs because these pants couldn't fit indoors. Historians have pointed out that one never sees black-and-white photos of a ranger in jodhpurs *and* carrying a backpack. Backpacks weren't needed when wearing jodhpurs. Useful items were stored in the extra large bulges of the pants. These items could include such things as water-proof matches or a pony.

Another fashion accessory associated with the Park Service is the flat "Smokey Bear" hat. The Park Service was truly a trend-setter with this stylish topper, but we didn't get there overnight. Original designs show that the Park Service tried many styles prior to the ultimate selection of the flat hat. Initially, there was the stovepipe model made popular by Abraham Lincoln. The Park Service made some minor modifications to the hat, which, as it turned out, was an actual stovepipe and could be used to channel smoke out of a log cabin (providing the ranger wasn't wearing jodhpurs and could get inside). This design proved unpopular because of rain. The damper within the pipe was always open; plus no one wants to wear a big electrical conductor on their head in a lightning storm. Another unpopular design was the beret. This gave the ranger a distinctly French demeanor, which caused them to smoke cigarettes, drink wine, and be rude to park visitors. Additionally, the beret is useless, even as a hat, and should only be used to clean up spills in the garage. Finally came the flat hat, which was stylish and useful. The first flat hat prototype was the graduation hat, or mortar-board. But that could only be worn with long flowing robes and, when combined with jodhpurs, made you look fat. Plus, the tassel had a tendency to obscure your vision. Then came the hat that we associate with the Park Service today, the Smokey Bear hat. It gave the ranger a look that park visitors would immediately recognize, a friendly look that said, "Pick up that litter–NOW!" but it also said, "This hat provides

shade for my face while I sleep in a flower-filled meadow."
Which, I think you'll agree, is quite a lot for any hat to say.

One of my favorite Park Service uniforms offered nowadays
is the "maternity suit." When a woman is pregnant there is a
glow about her; warm light radiates off of her vibrant skin.
With so many acres of wild beauty in national parks, we can't
have people looking at radiant childbearing women. Visitors
should look at the scenery, not pregnant people. So, it was
decided that we should cover up pregnant employees. The
Park Service has taken the *Wizard of Oz* approach in hiding
pregnant woman. It covered them in drapes (curtain rod
included to give that broad-shouldered look), as if to say, "Pay
no attention to the employee behind the curtain." There is no
denying that when a woman wears this stylish, pleated, gray
topper with green pants sporting a huge, elastic waistline, she
says to the world, in a loud, clear voice, "You can't see me."

When I first started working in Glacier, we couldn't wear
shorts. For years and years the cool comfort of shorts was
denied Park Service employees because it might give the
public the impression that we weren't sweating profusely. So,
we'd hike, mile after mile in our wool pants, sweating. However, some older, seasoned veterans were cool as cucumbers,
wearing their jodhpurs loaded with ice.

More recently, we've been allowed to wear shorts. The first
attempt at shorts was the "Daisy Duke" model (a.k.a. Park
Service "hot pants"). They were very short shorts that saved
the taxpayers thousands of dollars because very little cloth was
used in the making of them. These shorts had just a bit more
material than the now defunct Park Service thong (a.k.a. the

Park Service "banana hammock"), which was made with no fabric at all. Many people complained about the shortness of the Daisy Dukes and about the exposed skin. Initially, the Park Service managers did nothing about these complaints. But then the visiting public complained, too. They were grossed out. At this point, park managers did hear the cries and made some changes. It was time to lengthen the Daisy Dukes.

It must be noted that during this fashion epoch, Michael Jordan was making his impact upon the NBA's uniform; the NBA shorts went from shorts that covered the upper thigh to shorts that extended past the knee. This fashion went well past the boundaries of the NBA. So inspired, NPS uniform makers made their own version of these shorts, but since park employees are substantially shorter than NBA players, employees were wearing pants again. But they allowed us to cut them with scissors.

One strange phenomenon that is seldom mentioned about Park Service clothing is the magical fabric from which it is made. Depending upon the season, this mysterious fabric expands or contracts; your clothes get bigger or smaller. For example, when I hang up my hiking shorts for the season, I know all about them; I know exactly how they should feel. After hiking mile after mile each week, I know my shorts! But then, in the fall, I put them in a box until spring. There the fabric phenomenon takes place, within the secrecy of the box. In the darkness of the closet, they inexplicably begin to shrink. I think about that a lot during the winter when I've got nothing else to do except drink beer and write about fashion.

Anyway, when no one is looking, thread by thread, the tiny spaces in the fabric shrink. Shorts, pants, shirts—the whole green and gray wardrobe—has been seasonally shriveled.

Then, when you pull them out of the box in the spring, *they're too small.* Try as you might, you just can't make your butt go into your pants or shorts without some type of friction-reducing lubricant. And seeing as you used up your winter supply of butter on all the popcorn you ate, you are now forced to order new, larger pants, shorts, and shirts.

Now that your clothes have done the winter contractions, it's time for summer expansions. You begin your season in your new, larger pants or shorts. You get the feel of them as you hike day after day, mile after mile. Then, sometime in the middle of the summer, boom! your shorts suddenly expand. You have all these clothes that are now much too big. You remember the "too small" clothes boxed away in the closet and try them on. They too have expanded, and now you can fit into them without smearing on lubricant. They fit perfectly. Someone should look into this. I would, but right now I'm eating oodles of buttery popcorn.

Well, I hope you learned a little something about Park Service uniforms. It's a history with a checkered past and a bright, paisley future. But now is the time to take action. The NPS needs snappy uniforms! We should all write Congress and express our concerns. We can't have people running around in the woods with shrinking and expanding pants. It's much too dangerous. And the whole green-and-gray color scheme must be replaced by something more colorful,

Troubleshooting in Bear Country

The bear. Much has been written about this magnificent creature, but many of the writings are outdated, anti-quated, conflicting, contradictory, and redundant. Yet readers feel that "if it's in print, it must be true." They are often confused by this differing information because writers have blended fact with fiction or, worse, hearsay. With all this misunderstanding surrounding bears, I have taken it upon myself to add to it.

Glacier National Park's 1 million acres are home to a variety of bears. There is the American black bear (*Ursus darkgui*), the grizzly (*Ursus noncrossumpathi*), the elusive polar bear (*Ursus bigwhiti*) and the Chicago bear (*Champs thatlbethedae*). Only the grizzly and black bears are seen with any regularity. Both the polar and Chicago bears, though found in the park, can ironically only be seen when nobody is looking. Researchers studying these bears are stymied and have concentrated their efforts by getting jobs in accounting.

Regarding the other two bears, the grizzly and the black, there is still much confusion. Most of this confusion is due to a single attribute: color. Many people live in areas where black bears are, in fact, black. But in Montana, as well as other Rocky Mountain areas, black bears can be any color. Their color can be black, yes, but many black bears are blond, red, brown, and occasionally plaid. About the only place in Glacier National Park where all black bears are in fact black is in the dark.

The grizzly is the larger cousin (once removed on its mother's side) of the black bear. Many visitors to our national parks often see bears, but have trouble telling whether they are grizzlies or black bears. The following may aid people in telling what type of bear they are seeing—but, then again, it may not.

1. Grizzlies are larger than black bears and have a large muscular hump over their shoulders. This hump is a product of pulling on ropes to ring church bells in France, but it also aids the bear in obtaining food that is buried in the ground. Grizzlies eat roots, ground squirrels, and missing Mob informants.
2. Grizzlies will often be playing with shredded Patagonia clothing.
3. A time-honored tale has it that you can also tell which type of bear is following you by climbing a tree. A black bear will climb up after you, and a grizzly will simply shake you out.

Grizzlies have coexisted with black bears for centuries; in fact, grizzlies love black bears. "Tastes like chicken," one grizzly is reported to have said. But since many black bears don't want to end up as a grizzly's snack, these two species avoid close contact. Similar relationships can be found in many Hollywood homes.

In many national parks, humans and bears also coexist, which can be a precarious relationship indeed. In truly wild areas, one can never completely eliminate natural hazards, such as rain, rockslides, avalanches, and sudden swings in the mood of management. One must be prepared for any event in the wilderness, whether it is a rock rampaging down a mountain and striking you on the head or a bear rampaging down a mountain and striking you in the head. There is no way to guarantee safety in a government-controlled area. Be prepared and educate yourself, especially in bear country.

While hiking in grizzly country, it is wise to make your presence known. If they know you are hiking down the trail, bears often clear out of an area to let you pass. But you have to let the bear know you are coming. How? Make noise. Many people shout or clap their hands, but one of the most effective methods of clearing wildlife, or other hikers, off a trail is to sing any Céline Dion tune. (You can't do it ... unless you're Céline.)

One popular method of keeping a safe distance between yourself and a bear is to use bear bells. But many people have trouble placing them on the bears, so they opt to wear the bells themselves—on their shoes, backpack, or hiking stick.

Years of research have proven, beyond a shadow of a doubt, that wearing these bells will make even the most "bear-a-noid" hiker look silly. These fifty-cent bear bells can often be purchased for two dollars at convenience stores and out of the trunks of cars located throughout the area.

To further reduce the risks in bear country, you should never hike alone. There is an old cliché in bear country: "There is safety in numbers." Since bears can run about 30 miles per hour—even faster than Olympic sprinters fresh out of a pharmacy—one should choose very slow hiking companions. If a bear attack seems imminent, first push down a fellow hiker and then get out of the area. If your hiking companions have been chosen carefully, you should be safe, the bear will be well fed, and this year's vacation slide show will be the most gripping yet.

Recently, a new product has been placed on the market for hikers who wish to avoid encounters with bears. This product is a bear repellent. Bear repellent is capsicum, the substance that makes your mouth burn when you eat a jalapeño. It is also the substance that burns the day *after* you eat a jalapeño. Contrary to popular belief, bear repellent should not be applied in the same manner as mosquito repellent. Rather, it should be used when an aggressive bear charges. When a bear runs at you, pull out your bear repellent and spray it directly into the eyes of a fellow hiking companion (only discharge half of the can). This relieves you of the burden of actually having to push that person down. The spray should stop the charge unless the bear has developed a taste for Mexican food. If your friend has a sense of humor, you can later nervously laugh off the whole charging episode. If your friend is angry to the point of physical violence, use the remaining half of the can.

In the event of conflict with a bear, remember that the bear sees you as a threat and will treat you just like any other bear. How would another bear act? Submissively. If a bear runs at you, acting submissively may help the situation enormously. Get down, be small (given the circumstances, that should be easy ...), curl up into the fetal position, mesh your fingers behind your head and neck, place your head between your legs, and pucker up. Don't come out of this "submissive posture." Just wait. How long? Quite possibly, the rest of your life ... even the experts don't know.

The grizzly is reported to be one of the most intelligent animals on Earth. It ranks just below marine mammals and chimpanzees and just a hair above those in TV sitcoms. But with regard to intelligence, one thing is certain: once bears learn to obtain food from humans, there is going to be trouble. If a bear eats a Twinky at a picnic table, it will come back for more Twinkies (again, scientists are baffled).

Oddly enough, most problems associated with bears are caused by humans, not by bears. Glacier National Park, like a few other national parks, has an elite corps of rangers whose job it is to reduce human-bear encounters. They patrol trails and campgrounds looking for people who leave food unattended, coolers out, or generally messy campsites. In the event that these rangers find people who have indeed left their food unattended, they spring into action. A highly motivated, if underpaid bunch, they are the best of the best: the "Bear Management Rangers."

When they find a messy camp or unattended food, the Bear Management Rangers will find a hiding place a discreet distance from the site. When the offending party returns, they take aim with a gun that is loaded with a tranquilizing dart, and shoot. Boom! The messy camper goes down.

Shortly after injection, the campers who left their food out will succumb to the effects of the drug, and once asleep, the rangers carefully secure the area and approach.

They weigh the subject, pull a tooth to determine age, and place a numbered tag in the ear. Also, while the subject is out cold, they go through the subject's pockets (somebody really should do something to see that these rangers are better paid. ...)

Sometimes, the traveling habits of messy campers must be studied by someone with lots of letters after his or her name, who sees to it that a radio collar is placed around the neck of the mess-maker. In this new management plan, scientists track the movements of the miscreant, and all the information is then recorded and sent to the Bureau of Endless Paper, in Washington, D.C., where it is promptly made into confetti.

Oftentimes, the darted subject is recognized as a repeat offender. This tagged person has caused trouble and left food out before. The ecosystem just can't afford to have people making messes and teaching bears about human food. So, the offender will have to be removed from the ecosystem. But it is a humane removal. The bear rangers pull yet another tooth and relocate the perpetrator to an area where he or she will blend in perfectly. If you look carefully, you may see bear rangers bringing in an unconscious form to monster truck rallies, hockey games, and other places where teeth are few.

All this constitutes bear management. Keeping the bear away from human food reduces the chances of a human-bear conflict and makes our national parks much safer places to visit.

So, go out and hike! Don't let "bear-a-noia" keep you from hiking the trails. Yes, bears are out there, but just keep in mind that they are the fastest, largest, land-dwelling meat eaters— and they are always hungry, but you should be okay.* As you hike Montana's backcountry, you will undoubtedly encounter local charlatans who consider themselves experts on bear behavior. You must recognize that these "experts" are just plain nuts who enjoy passing on misinformation. You should be responsible for educating yourself, trust your instincts, and remember that the opinion you should listen to is mine.

---

* maybe

Some Like It Hot

Since Glacier National Park abuts Waterton National Park in Canada, you may find yourself crossing the border. One sure way to make the guys at a Canadian customs station smile is to play a little joke on them when entering their country. As your car pulls up to the gate, it is the duty of the customs official to ask you some questions, such as, "Are you bringing any oranges or citrus products into Canada?" Tell them, "Absolutely not." Canadian officials are worried about oranges and rightfully so; it is well documented that in the wrong hands, oranges can be extremely dangerous. People have been known to enter Canadian convenience stores, brandishing oranges, threatening people, and robbing the place at "orange point." Why? Because Canadians don't allow guns or pepper spray. Then, when the customs guy asks you, "Do you have any guns or pepper spray?" tell them, "Absolutely. Which do you need?" They always laugh at that one. They will think you are so witty they will keep you around all day and, to show their appreciation, give you, absolutely free, a total body cavity search before sending you back stateside.

It's not just customs officials. Most people I know find a lot of humor in pepper spray. For the uninitiated, pepper spray is used while hiking in areas that have bears. Both black and grizzly bears can be aggressive at times and might charge if they see humans as a threat. If you are hiking, and a grizzly charges, pull out your pepper spray and spray it in its face. This Tabasco-like substance will enrage the already maddened animal, but it will also temporarily blind it. While the angry, sightless animal frantically thrashes the air with its long claws, you can hopefully make your escape. The curious may want to see what happens when the bruin regains its sight, but the wise are never so inquisitive.

You may ask, "What about guns?" Pepper spray has never been documented to stop a charging gun. But if people carry guns into areas with aggressive grizzlies and happen to shoot a charging grizzly, that is certain to make the bear very, very mad, indeed. But this time, it can still see you, and in its infuriated state, it will give chase. While running away, you may try to shoot back at the pursuing bear over your shoulder, Annie Oakley–style. And if you are Annie Oakley, you may hit your target. If not, well, consider pepper spray next time ... if there is a next time. Besides ... guns aren't allowed in the Park, anyway.

What comes next will be a bit of a departure for me because I want to relay a couple of incidents that actually occurred. No kidding; it really happened. But due to the fact that I lie, fib, stretch the truth, and speak in fluent hyperbole as often as possible, the reader may assume that I'm lying again or that I am possibly sick. In this case, I'm telling the truth, and the doctor says I should be "right as rain" and lying on my feet soon enough.

Pepper spray has been on the market for years, but I started to carry it only recently. The spray comes in a small can and also has a holster that can be placed upon your belt or backpack. Covering the "trigger" is a plastic guard—a safety—to keep the spray from going off unintentionally. I keep my pepper spray right on my belt, over my right front pocket, for quick access. I'm quite familiar with pepper spray and its effects, having used it myself once. While bushwhacking off trail, I was climbing a small cliff. I had both hands securely on a rock above me, and as I brought my leg up to a point of purchase, my abs—which have a pudding-like consistency and were hanging in several folds over my belt—made contact with the pepper spray can. The raising of my leg pushed it further into the folds of my flesh. Well, unbeknownst to me, the safety had been wrenched free during my trek through the thick brush. The lever depressed, releasing a jet of orange mist up into my eyes. Finding the humor in this situation, I laughed and laughed while tears of mirth streamed down my face. I was in such a jolly mood that I took this opportunity to invent new and colorful cusswords. I also used this time to bring out my lunch, which I had eaten about half an hour earlier. The stinging in my eyes lasted for over an hour, and the coughing lasted for days. But that really wasn't the worst part.

All that hot pepper permeated the fabric of my shirt and was burning the skin of my vanilla pudding chest and belly. I needed to wash the fiery pepper off, so naturally, I headed for the shower. Big mistake. Yes, I did remove some of the pepper from my belly, but then all that hot, burning pepper sauce was carried by the running water to my all-too-tender "nether regions," and no amount of soap or water could stop the burning. It was as though I had a hundred riled hornets stinging my crotch. Truly, it was the most painful hot, burning shower I ever took; and I was using cold water. Luckily for me, the pain went away after a few days, but I still had to guide hikes in the meantime. Visitors seemed to enjoy my John Wayne–like gait, commenting that there was enough room between my legs to accommodate a pregnant horse. I got off lucky. Bunky had it much worse.

Bunky was my roommate while I was stationed up at St. Mary. He was as smart a character as I've ever come across. Together, we were a study in contrast. He was the epitome of the Park Service figure: tall, dark, and handsome, with a ready smile. I, on the other hand, looked like an escapee from the Home for the Visually Unpleasant. With all my years of experience, I tried to teach Bunky, a rookie, about guiding hikes. But he discarded all my teachings, saying he wanted to do things his way and give "accurate information." He cut quite a figure in his green and gray uniform. He was knowledgeable, friendly, enthusiastic, charismatic, and hard working. Park visitors were just naturally, magnetically drawn to him. They saw him as a true ranger, a real hero.

One day when Bunky was working up at Logan Pass, visitors reported a grizzly very near the trail. Logan Pass is an area known for its mountain goat watching. Goats come from miles around to gawk at the thousands upon thousands of visitors hiking the trail. But to have a grizzly reported in an area with so many visitors gets a ranger's attention quickly. A grizzly in such an area can cause pandemonium, chaos, injury, or worse, people chasing the grizzly trying to get that "once-in-a-lifetime" (frequently referred to as "end-of-your-lifetime") snapshot.

Upon hearing the news, Bunky took charge of the potentially dangerous situation. He assembled the available park personnel, including Bear Rangers, and made a plan that integrated closure of the trail, evacuation of the boardwalk to Hidden Lake, and a trail sweep of the entire area. Bunky would "sweep" the trail, which meant he would go to the end of the trail and move all park visitors back toward the safety of Logan Pass Visitor Center. He would, of course, be carrying pepper spray to protect himself and park visitors from the threat of a grizzly attack. This plan had only two flaws: pepper spray and park visitors.

Bunky quickly hiked to Hidden Lake overlook; a mile and a half with about 700 feet of elevation gain. Hundreds of excited people were now coming down on their own, but Bunky was in charge of gathering all who remained at the overlook and escorting them down to the trailhead safely. Once he reached the overlook, he assembled all the lingering people. They were mostly foreign, from some eastern European country, and didn't speak English very goodly. Through gestures and stilted communication, Bunky told them of the situation and started to shepherd them down, all the while staying in the back of the group to keep anyone from straying. He was their hero. The ranger who saved them from the bear.

As they walked toward the visitors center, a few pulled out their cameras and took pictures of the heroic, smiling ranger ushering them to safety. Bunky was comforted by the fact that a few of the visitors were carrying pepper spray as well as cameras. "Can't have too many people carrying pepper spray today," he thought, but he was wrong.

Suddenly, from behind the group, sprinting as though their lives depended upon it, came a small group of mountain goats. The goats passed the people like a Ferrari passing an overheated Yugo. Bunky thought, "Wow! There's something you don't see every day: Sprinting goats ..."

People often say, in situations like that, that the hair on the back of their neck will raise, warning bells go off inside their heads, or they "just had a feeling something wasn't right." Whatever it was, Bunky knew before he turned around. He knew what was causing those normally unflappable goats to sprint. He knew what was driving them forward. Internally, something primal clicked, and he understood. Question and answer came at the same time. "What could be so horrible that it would make a goat dash like that?" Apparently the whole group went through a similar question-and-answer process because the whole group, in unison, turned their heads. The answer was approaching fast.

As Bunky turned around, he saw a huge, blond grizzly galumphing to a stop. Three hundred pounds of hide, fur, teeth, and claws going from a 35-mile-per-hour sprint to a skidding halt. According to Bunky, the look on the bear's face was one of "Whoa. Didn't expect that! People!" Bunky could read the animal well. It was only about 15 feet away. Now, when *I* face a situation where a bear comes dashing towards one of *my* groups, I tell the group to remain calm and quickly form a tight impenetrable circle around me, with small, chewy children on the outermost edge. But, as I mentioned earlier, Bunky threw out almost all of my lessons. This time it would cost him. Quite unintentionally, he was between an excited grizzly and his escorted group.

Very calmly, with nerves of steel, Bunky slowly went for his pepper spray. He watched the animal as he removed the holster's Velcro strap. Then he was suddenly hit. But it wasn't the frontal assault he'd expected. He was hit from behind.

Not by the bear, but pepper spray. Someone in *his* group sprayed him.

Just before Bunky could pull his pepper spray, he heard a "whoosh" and was enveloped in an orange-red mist. The toxic cloud hit him directly in the back of the head and then curled around to run a burning rake across his eyes and claw at his throat and lungs. He fell into a fetal position clutching his burning face in his hands. Blinded, coughing, gagging, and rolling on the ground, with an excited grizzly just a few feet away, he was helpless.

Now at this point, for the ladies, I must make something perfectly clear. Men have known this for ages, but women tend to forget. There is little difference between pain and anger to a man. The two are so closely woven together that they cannot be separated. For men, pain and anger make a legendary combination, like pizza and beer. The two just belong together.

That is why, when a man is hammering a nail and accidentally strikes his thumb, he shouts, "AMPERSAND–POUND SIGN–PERCENTAGE–ASTERISK!" (more commonly expressed as "&#%*!") or "EXPLETIVE!" or something similar and reacts as though he is angry. You'd think he'd just be in pain, but no, he's infuriated, too. Pain and anger just naturally go together. Only one thing could make the anger associated with the pain worse, and that's when it is caused by someone else's pepper spray.

"WHO THE EXPLETIVE SPRAYED THEIR POUND SIGN PEPPER SPRAY?" yelled Bunky between coughing fits and throwing up.

Someone from the group, probably the brave one who actually sprayed him, said very authoritatively, in his native tongue, "Umm ..."

"I CAN'T BELIEVE YOU EXPLETIVE SPRAYED ME ..."

"Umm ..."

After long, agonizing minutes of cursing and cussing that could paint the whole of Logan Pass blue, Bunky noticed that it was strangely quiet. He no longer heard the quiet, cautious "Umm ..." or any other sound for that matter. There was no rustle of fabric in the wind or of feet shuffling in gravel. Nothing. The silence was eerie.

"Better get it together," Bunky thought. "These people are stunned into silence. And, to them, I represent the whole Park Service." He took a few minutes to collect himself, gather his thoughts, and resume his task of escorting this group of foreigners back to the visitor center and to safety. When he finally pried his burning eyes open, he looked to the area where the bear had been—nothing. He turned and looked toward where his group had been—no one. Apparently, both bear and visitors were quite put off to hear such foul language. The bear leaving was understandable, but his group had left him there, blinded and helpless, a sacrificial ranger. He was all alone.

"Expletive," he said calmly.

Later, back at our Park Service hovel, Bunky relayed the story to me. His eyes were still red, and his voice was raspy. But the smile was there, and his zeal for life didn't seem to be affected. Only an hour or so after the incident, he was able to smile and laugh about it. We sat at the table, he told me the tale, and we giggled. Pepper spray and eastern European visitors are a bad combo. After the laughter, Bunky decided he'd take a shower to get the pepper spray out of his hair. He excused himself and went into the bathroom. I remember the sound of the running water, the sound of the shower curtain being drawn, and then the screams of pain.

I continued to giggle.

Predator Puma

There are few creatures in the animal kingdom that captivate the imagination like the mountain lion. As a predator it has few rivals, unless you include Hugh Hefner or Woody Allen. With its stealth, cunning, and charisma, the mountain lion holds us enthralled. But mountain lions are elusive, and not many of us actually have an opportunity to view one. Seeing a mountain lion is something precious and rare, sort of like finding a polite person in Paris, France.

Mountain lions (frequently called catamounts, panthers, cougars, pumas, and, occasionally, Nikes) are predators—meat eaters. Their diet consists of deer, elk, moose, and, if available, those little cocktail weenies. Like many members of the cat family, mountain lions are nocturnal, or active at night, and so much of their life remains a mystery. And their lives will continue to be a mystery as long as mountain lion researchers conduct their work during the day. Researchers have avoided working nights for various reasons, ranging from "It is difficult to write notes in the dark" to "It is difficult to write notes in the dark with this big cat on my chest."

Years ago, I had the pleasure of volunteering a few months of my precious time at a remote cabin in the Northfork region of Glacier National Park. Most people only dream of enjoying the solitude of a cabin in the middle of nowhere. Instead, each day they slave away at their 9-to-5 job, counting paperclips, chatting over coffee, and fantasizing about their escape into the freedom of the wild. But for me it was no fantasy, I was actually THERE ... because I didn't *have* a job.

The one-room cabin where I was stationed was built around 1900. The old log structure was situated in a small meadow used as a recreational facility by some of the resident deer. Hauling gear from the car to the cabin was about a quarter-mile trek, and I had so much gear I needed to make several trips. The deer were not disturbed by my activity in the least. They continued to frolic, playing games of "eat the flower" and "follow the butterfly," as I lugged provisions. I had left suburbia and entered a Disney fantasy.

The windows of the cabin were barred with iron and barbed wire to protect the cabin's contents from pesky forms of wildlife, such as mountain lions, grizzlies, wolverines, and campers who have run out of instant oatmeal. In front was a small porch that overlooked a lake. Downwind was the bathroom equipped with all the modern conveniences, such as a hole, a splintered wooden seat, corncobs, and a small amount of chlorinated lime. I thought the outhouse was kind of fun, in a primitive sort of way. But on future trips I'd forgo the rustic pleasures and bring some toilet tissue, two-ply.

My first morning, after a warm spring rain, I decided to take a 6-mile hike up to the head of the lake and check out the backcountry campground. Since I was a lowly volunteer, I wanted to show the "powers that be" that I had some initiative. Besides, I wanted to see if the outhouse at the other end of the lake had any toilet paper to swipe.

As I was walking up the muddy trail, numerous deer tracks reminded me that I wasn't alone in my wilderness world. Signs of deer were everywhere: scat (a scientific term meaning "Shoo! Go away!"), tracks, and plant limbs that had a ragged appearance due to feeding. Although a novice in these woods, I knew that where there are deer, there are also predators. Fearing that there was a predator ready to separate me from my viscera, I became acutely aware of my surroundings; my personal radar was turned on and set on high. Sounds that normally went undetected seemed amplified; my eyes picked up on odd colors and things that seemed out of place; subtle movements quickly drew my attention. I kept sniffing for strange scents. If animals were going to eat me, first they had to invade the protective umbrella of my heightened senses. Then, quite suddenly, I felt a squishing sensation oozing from either side of my right foot. I had stepped into some warm—I believe the scientific word for it is—poop, and I also made a mental note to check the warranty on my personal radar.

I took off my backpack and hunkered down to inspect the poop. I pulled out my field guides, pored over the pages, and found out, with certainty, that this discovery wasn't a ruby throated hummingbird or a glacier lily. After consulting a book on tracking, I narrowed the substance down to mountain lion poop. I was thrilled—and a little scared.

Knowing that I was walking in the same vicinity as a mountain lion put a spring in my step. I was about a mile from the backcountry campground and, due to said spring, I made it in three paces.

Seeing the campground made me feel more secure. After walking 6 miles and finding no apparent traces of humans, this backcountry site was quite a relief. Signs of humanity were everywhere. The trees had been thinned, there were leveled areas for tents, and an outhouse loomed as large as a skyscraper. All these signs of human occupancy slowed my heart's frantic pace.

Feeling somewhat courageous again, I decided to have a look about the campground. I inspected all the tent sites individually, hoping to find signs of upright animals. A short examination of the whole area told me I had the whole valley to myself. Not so much as an old piece of garbage or a tent peg could be found. There were no tracks in the fresh mud, human or otherwise. The only prints to be found in the muddy campground were mine.

Soon, I realized that I was in the same area as the outhouse, or as we like to say euphemistically in the Park Service, a "comfort station." There is a law of nature that states that how badly one needs to use the comfort station is directly proportional to how close one is to the actual relief site. A great distance means no great need; a close distance, however, has some urgency attached. I'm not one to break laws, especially laws of nature, and I needed some comfort. Besides, maybe I could acquire the much-needed toilet paper.

As I walked toward the comfort station, I hit the side of my head with the heel of my right hand just to see if I could jump-start my faulty radar. I could almost hear it turn on with a chug and a sputter, and if someone else had been around, they might have been able to hear it too.

Radar on. Check. Sniff and sample the air—nothing; check. Listen for unusual sounds—nothing; check. Look for tracks near the outhouse—nothing; check. Enter outhouse; check. Discontinue air sampling, quickly; check. Look for toilet paper; *be damned sure and* check. Obey laws of nature; check. Relax and shut off radar; check.

Naturally, I was much relieved upon coming out of the outhouse. Good thing, too. As I was zipping up my fly, I looked down into the mud. Directly in front of my boot, about a foot away, there was a large set of distinctive, four-toed tracks: mountain lion. Muddy water could be seen *seeping into* and filling up the imprints. Fresh! If I hadn't, only seconds ago, been following the laws of nature, I would certainly be following them now.

In a desperate attempt to activate my radar, I started frantically hitting my head again. The air was still and silent, but the tracks, which circled the outhouse, indicated a mountain lion—here—*NOW!* I scanned the nearby trees, the top of the biffy, all around. My heart rate steadily increased.

I thought to myself, "When would be a good time to leave?" Under the circumstances, "NOW!" seemed to be a reasonable answer. I started back the 6 miles, toward the safety of the cabin, when I realized that my fresh tracks leading up to the campground had been stepped on by the same four-toed tracks. The mountain lion had followed me up to the campsite.

Getting back to the cabin was the longest, most difficult hike I have ever experienced. My entire body shook with fear. I couldn't rely on my defective radar to protect me from an animal whose survival is based on stealth. Then I remembered something I read about protecting yourself from mountain lions: If one encounters a menacing mountain lion, one should look directly at it ... make eye contact. I had to continuously scan the entire area. But since I had no idea from which direction the mountain lion would come, I had to check all possibilities and rotate 360 degrees. So, flushed with adrenaline, I hiked by pirouetting, like a whirling dervish, the entire way back to the cabin. Let's see him walk in my footsteps now!

I stopped only once, and that was to check on a French couple hiking the same trail. They must have seen something coming down the trail, possibly the mountain lion, that caused them considerable alarm. They leaped off the trail as I came spinning toward them. Due to the language barrier, I couldn't tell what they were trying to communicate by rotating their index fingers around their ears. It could have been French sign language.

Once back at the cabin, I threw myself on the soft green grass and waited for my heart to stop racing and for the world to stop spinning. The cabin, the trees, and one resident deer were all revolving around me at an incredible rate. Pirouetting a trail for 6 miles is great aerobic exercise, but it can make one just a little dizzy. After a short time, the world ceased to spin and returned to normal. As I sat up in the cool breeze, I ran a hand across my sweaty brow and looked ahead. My blood froze. Ten feet away, a mountain lion crouched, ready to spring upon me as though I were stuffed with catnip. After spinning down that trail, I was stuffed with absolutely nothing. A fact the mountain lion should have noticed as he followed me.

As the mountain lion faced me, I became mesmerized by the pale, yellow-green depths of its eyes; the pupils grew larger and larger. Its claws sunk into the soft soil. Like a Looney Tunes character, I could see the large cat envisioning me as some oversized cocktail weenie. And what a weenie I was.

I watched the tawny cat's haunches wiggle in anticipation of the deadly pounce. As the tensed feline leaped, a scream escaped from my lips. It was so high that no one actually heard it. (Though, strangely, far away some wolves broke into a howl.) I sat frozen, watching this mountain lion sail, slow-motion, through the air, while I sat forcing air out through my gaping, silent orifice. I was still soundlessly screaming, too. I closed my eyes. I heard the cat land. A guttural snarl. I heard a strange bleating sound. I felt nothing. No pain. No pain.

It had just attacked one of the resident deer.

It was over quickly for the deer. It was over quickly for me, as a witness. Very nimbly, and with strength that belied its size, the cat dragged the carcass away into the trees. Just like that—it was over.

Sweating and shaking, I hauled myself out of the grass. My quivering bones wouldn't totally support my weight, and I staggered over to the cabin. I was dizzy again. I threw open the door, saw my bed, and collapsed. A few more steps, and I would have actually landed on the bed. The floor felt cool on my face. I closed my eyes and drifted, mercifully, into slumber.

The next morning I awoke, still on the floor. The sunlight that streamed through the barred windows bounced off a little puddle of drool on the floor, reflecting directly into my eyes. I pushed myself off the floor and got up on my feet. One advantage of sleeping on the floor is that making the bed takes no time. I wiped the drool up with a hankie. I squinted toward the light. It was a bright sunny day. It held a lot of potential.

As I moved, my muscles responded slowly and felt stiff, calling to mind yesterday's events. I made myself some instant oatmeal and gingerly walked down to the lake. At the shore, I faced the sun and felt the warm reflections off the water illuminating my face. The sun was well over the peaks, and I knew I had slept in, but I didn't care. I looked out over the lake, which was as smooth as polished glass. I thought about the previous day. The big thrill. I had finally seen my first mountain lion! My feet started to shuffle. I couldn't help it; I started to dance. At the water's edge, I happily twirled about like a whirling dervish.

Life Ain't da Pits

S ome people seem to lead charmed lives. I recognize that I have absolutely no charm, but I know I'm a lucky person. People will come right up to me and tell me how fortunate I am to work for the National Park Service in Glacier National Park. Imagine working in an area with incredible scenery: majestic peaks, crystal clear waters, and visitors clad in vibrant hues of polyester. How wonderful to be able to work surrounded by a million acres of wild beauty.

But it's not all a bed of roses. Today's Park Service's budget isn't what it once was. It used to be thin; now it's anorexic. So there are a couple of drawbacks working here: (1) the low pay and (2) working for peanuts. Yet, in spite of this, park visitors often tell me that they would like to trade places. They would like to give up their high-paying job for a low-paying, seasonal job like mine. They, too, would like to work for peanuts. I'm not sure, but I think this is what psychologists call "peanuts envy."

In my line of work, I talk with hundreds of visitors each day. One of the most frequently asked questions is, "How can I get a job like yours?" It's ironic that they would envy my work when the fact that I'm walking around in my bare feet demonstrates that I don't make a lot of money.

We all remember certain events in our lives that make our existence so much better. One such time was when a very well-to-do person (in the same tax bracket as Bill Gates) told me how lucky I was to love my work. That incident will always be with me.

One hot August day, I was digging an outhouse pit for a new privy at one of Glacier's more isolated campgrounds. It was 90 degrees in the shade, and the nearest shade, according to the weather person, was in Seattle. My green-and-gray polyester uniform was drenched with sweat and sticking to my body. As I threw dirt over my shoulder, I heard the purring sound of a powerful, well-tuned engine. Like a ground squirrel, I peeped out of my chest-high pit to see what was approaching.

My pupils constricted to mere pinpoints as they were hit with a dazzling light. The sun was shining directly upon a gleaming emerald-green Jaguar XJS$. Spoked wheels, polished chrome, and personalized plates that read "RICHRNU" adorned the car. It pulled up, and the purring engine was silenced.

An impeccably groomed man, about my own age, stepped from the roadster. He was wearing a white suit made entirely of natural fibers. His wingtip shoes gave off their own light, and his gold and diamond pinky ring mirrored their brilliance. He was a sparkly man. As he walked toward me,

I became all too aware of my own grungy appearance. Embarrassed, I slunk into the depths of the outhouse pit, hoping he would pass by. He didn't.

"Excuse me, Sir. But whatever are you doing?" he asked, articulating each word clearly.

"Wadja' say?" I answered.

"Ah, a native," he murmured under his breath. He started over. "'Skuse me. "Wadja' doin' there?"

"Oh, jus' digg'n' a new pit fer an outhouse," I said throwing more dirt over my shoulder.

"Oh," said Well-Groomed Man, surveying the scene. He was silent a while, then asked, "Wouldn't a shovel make the diggin' easier?"

I went into a lengthy discourse about the Park Service's budget and how we could no longer afford frilly things like shovels, so we just used our hands. He seemed sympathetic: "At least they pay you by the hour."

Pulling a large red silk hanky from his breast pocket, Well-Groomed Man spread it out on the lip of the outhouse pit. Though somewhat intimidated by his appearance, I nevertheless climbed out of the pit to be more sociable, and to share some of my hard-earned peanuts. Besides, I needed to pick rocks out from under my fingernails. There we sat, a study in contrast.

As we dangled our feet into the pit and talked, I came to understand how he could afford such a nice suit and fine car. His name was Donald Rockefeller Carnegie Hill Turner Trump, and his was a family steeped in traditional old money. He said that he was an attorney and his hobbies were real estate development and competitive yachting. His was a very stressful life, and on the recommendation of one of his therapists (he wasn't sure which one), he was instructed to "get away from it all and unwind." Personally, I thought it curious that anyone with enough money to purchase Fiji could feel hypertension.

During our conversation, I began to see how the other half lived. I had never been out of Montana and had yet to see the outside world (something for which I'm still thankful). But Well-Groomed Man told me he was tired, disillusioned, and frustrated with the fast pace and the materialism so prevalent in his world. He was fed up with friends who were always comparing vintage cars, mansions (his, by the way, was recently featured in the magazine *Better Homes Than Yours*), and other status symbols.

"Status symbols?" I inquired. "You mean like a ... popcorn popper?"

He looked at me and smiled; it was a smile I had trouble interpreting.

Then Well-Groomed Man said something that indicated he suffered from an acute case of peanuts envy: "I'd give anything to be in your shoes." I politely informed him I wasn't wearing any shoes, just several layers of dirt.

"No," he responded, "that's not what I mean. You are one lucky man. Here you are, surrounded by truly wild beauty. You live among the grizzlies in rugged snow-capped mountains. You walk out your door and listen to the music of the wolf, the wind, or waterfalls. You have it all. ..." His words hung in the air as he looked at his wingtip shoes. "All I have in my world is money and the pressure that comes with it—pressure with a capital P. I'd give anything for a job like yours."

I looked past my dirty toes into the pit. Then, I looked at Well-Groomed Man, then back at the pit. Not one to miss an opportunity, I told him I had an idea.

Well, all that stress that Well-Groomed Man was feeling seemed to disappear as the pit grew deeper. He went at it like a professional outhouse digger. He only stopped once, to take off his pinky ring.

Not one to shirk my duties, I stayed at the edge of the pit and supervised and offered words of encouragement, such as, "Watch where you throw that dirt, this uniform is real polyester," or "Can I drive your car?" Because he wasn't working for an hourly wage, the pit was finished in record time.

I helped him out of the pit and offered him some of my water and popcorn. He gladly accepted the water but politely declined the popcorn, saying he preferred his actually popped.

"Ya know," he said, "I've never felt better in my whole life."

"Me either."

We stood at the edge of the pit and admired our work. As far as outhouse pits go, it was a beauty. Certainly good enough for its intended use. He broke the silence, brushing the dust off his sleeves. "C'mon, I'll drive you home."

He dropped me off at the door of my Park Service hovel. After taking the protective plastic cover off the passenger seat, he offered me his card and said I should feel free to call him if I needed some legal advice or was looking to purchase some land or a used yacht. He slapped me on the back and stated that he had never had such a wonderful time.

"I've just got to tell my therapists about this. I'm going to recommend this to all my friends," he said.

"Please do," I responded eagerly, thinking of all the pits I had yet to dig. I was secretly hoping "peanuts envy" would be hitting epidemic proportions.

He climbed back into his Jaguar and sped off into the setting sun. I stood at the door of my hovel and watched the dust rise from his ever-fading wheels. As the purr of his engine diminished, my attention was drawn to the jagged peaks silhouetted against a crimson sky. In the distance I heard the low thunder of a waterfall. I looked at my hands. I noticed how clean they were.

You know, I am pretty lucky.

Aliens on Vacation

"There is no such thing as a stupid question." I hear that dogmatic phrase a lot. Each year during our training seminars, we rangers sit with our legs folded in a lotus position, eyes closed, and chant our mantra: "Ohoooom. There is no such thing as a stupid question. Ohoooom." I heard it my first year and every year since. I'll hear it again in my next training session. In the early years, the "no such thing as a stupid question" mantra made perfect sense; visitors should ask their questions, speak their minds, and we, as rangers, should encourage questions. But as I became more experienced, I also became more suspicious. I've had questions asked of me, that, if they weren't stupid, were very closely related, possibly Stupid's first inbred cousin. Having experienced such questions, during training I'd sit in the lotus position, chanting, but I'd cheat. I'd open one eye and peek at the other rangers.

Have they ever been asked a stupid question? I couldn't be the only one. Could my supervisors, with all their years of accumulated wisdom, be wrong? Are "stupid questions" out there? As I sat peeking, I noticed a few "older" rangers sneaking a peek too. They had their eyes open and were shifting around. That lotus position sure is uncomfortable, and after a couple of years on the job, so is the mantra.

As a disposable, er, I mean, seasonal employee, one of the things I've learned is that permanents, who do all the hiring, are "right." It doesn't matter what the subject is, they are "right" and not to be questioned, especially by a dispo ... seasonal employee. Seasonals are not to argue because it could cost them their job if they raise a question or cause other problems. I've seen seasonals who question permanent employees, and the next season, mysteriously, those seasonal employees don't return. They just vanish into the ether—and so do their questions. So I know, beyond a shadow of a doubt, that when my supervisors, who are permanent and control my employment fate, say that there are "no stupid questions," I don't object. At least not without facts.

I've done some deep investigative work into the "stupid question" phenomenon (I read the *Weekly World News* while waiting in line at the grocer's). What I found was startling. My bosses were right (as usual) ... people don't ask stupid questions. Aliens do.

Aliens, extraterrestrials, little green men, or whatever you want to call them, are visiting our national parks—and *they* are asking stupid questions. On the surface, these questions may seem inane and out of place, but as we probe deeper, we find that they are, in fact, dumb. They are not the type of questions *people* would ask. No, people are far too smart to ask such things, but aliens, who are not familiar with our customs, idiom, and culture, might just ask stupid questions. I base this, not only on my extensive research of the *Weekly World News*, but also on some well-documented hearsay and the *X-Files*.

Almost 100 percent of the questions I receive are normal, nonstupid questions—questions so relevant and pertinent they just go unnoticed—they fit right in, blend into the scenery, and go perfectly with the day's hike: What's that flower? Why are the rocks red? What's your sign? But aliens ask questions that are difficult, if not impossible, to answer. I'm not saying aliens will ask you hard math questions, such as what's the square root of pi, but they ask questions that stand out.

Let's say, for example, I stop along the trail and get all excited because I see a fresh bolete mushroom has popped up. I mention how delicious and highly prized the bolete is and how it is easily distinguished from other mushrooms because it doesn't have gills under the cap. Let's say, for example, at that point, someone, an alien in the guise of a human, asks, "Why don't they serve mushroom soup at the cafeteria any more?"

I don't want this person to hold back or even think the question was stupid (might be human; alien disguises are so good), so I remain polite and encourage them to clarify their question.

"What are you talking about, Zebop?!" I ask through a smile.

"I like soup." the alien says. "Mushroom soup. But they don't serve it anymore at the cafeteria. I thought you might know why?"

"No, I don't know," I say after a long pause. I'm a little at a loss for words, but I still try to connect with them. "I like mushroom soup, too."

The alien then looks nervously at the normal, human park visitors, shifting its gaze to the right and to the left. The other human visitors just stare in stunned silence, not knowing what to say. The alien, sensing the awkwardness and knowing its cover has been blown, plans its escape. A beam of light illuminates the alien, and it begins to dissolve and break down to a molecular level and is magically teleported, or "beamed up," to the mother ship. Visitors don't ask stupid questions; aliens do.

Aliens don't show up every day. In fact, they don't even show up once a week. But about once a year, they make their presence known through their inane questions or even their actions. For example, at Logan Pass, there are thousands upon thousands of Columbian ground squirrels. Due to an unnatural diet of Twinkies, Cheez Doodles, and lard blobs, many of these ground squirrels have attained the size of large furry pillows.

I once saw an alien try to feed a cream-filled Cheeze-Zit to a squirrel at Logan Pass, and in a national park, feeding wildlife is strictly forbidden—especially feeding them items with "yellow number 5" listed as a top ingredient. As an emissary of the National Park Service, I politely informed the alien that this action, this feeding, was illegal.

"Excuse me, Zoltar, but you should not feed squirrels in the park," I said.

"Uhh, I didn't know it was a squirrel." he said, pulling back his Cheeze-Zit, "I thought I was feeding a pillow."

"No, on Earth, pillows don't eat. It's a squirrel," I said, "and we ask that visitors refrain from feeding wildlife."

"I like Earth life forms," he added with a smile. "They're cute and made of long carbon chains."

"Umm ... Yes. Please don't feed wildlife. Thank you."

Zoltar ate the cheese substitute substance himself but was still fascinated by the ground squirrel. Pulling out his car keys, he dangled them in front of the squirrel. At this, I was shocked: Aliens have car keys! The squirrel, too, must have sensed some peril, possibly an impending Earth invasion, and grabbed the alien's keys and carried them deep down its hole. It never returned the keys.

That squirrel taught the alien a lesson much more effectively than I ever could. The lesson was: "Don't mess with Earthlings, or they will take your keys!" The alien looked at me, as though I could help control the squirrel's behavior and magically make his keys reappear. I just shrugged. I could see his anger grow, but before he could take out his laser gun and start blasting craters all over Logan Pass, a beam of light came down and teleported Zoltar back to the mother ship. That was years ago, but I'm sure that mother ship is still quietly orbiting the planet; we still have the keys, and I keep getting stupid questions.

Over the years, I've kept a list of questions that indicate we are being observed by an alien race. I did not make these up. These are very real questions that I've become aware of either first- or secondhand. I've decided to share them with other humans so that they can also identify aliens and thus protect both the park and Earth. I've even come up with answers to keep the aliens flummoxed and befuddled so that they don't invade us anytime soon.

Here then, are some very real questions asked by alien visitors to Glacier National Park:

Alien: "At what altitude does a deer become an elk?"

Ranger: "Approximately 2,000 feet, or higher if they have ambition and want to become a moose."

Alien: "When do the glaciers move?"

Ranger: *(checking his watch)* "3:30—Oh darn! You know ... you just missed it. Try again tomorrow."

Alien: "What do you do with the animals at night?"

Ranger: "Why, at night, we herd them all up and lock them in their cages, where they are fed a protein-rich diet of extraterrestrials."

Alien: "Does this lake go all the way to the bottom?"

Ranger: "Oddly enough, it doesn't. There is a huge air-filled gap between the water and the bottom. It's where we conduct tests on our experimental weapons."

Alien: "How much does that mountain weigh?"

Ranger: "Nothing. It's not a mountain, it's a helium balloon, and if it weren't anchored, it would float around. You've probably seen that mountain in the Macy's Thanksgiving Day Parade while monitoring Earth's TV transmissions."

Alien: "How many undiscovered caves are there in the park?"

Ranger: "There are exactly thirteen undiscovered caves within the park. We charted their whereabouts, but then we forgot where we put the chart. This 'forgetting' is a dominate gene in humans. We are a forgetful race and should not interbreed with aliens."

Alien: *(pointing at snow high up on mountain)* "That's not snow ... can't be snow. It's shaped just like a '57 Chevy."

Ranger: "Strangely enough, it is a Chevy, a '56. It's been there for years. But the real strange thing is, each spring, it gets a tune-up and has a new coat of wax."

Alien: "Did this park used to be Yellowstone?"

Ranger: "Yes, and next year we are going to be Banff. Earth is a very unstable planet."

Alien: "At the end of the rut, doesn't an elk's head fall off?"

Ranger: "No, their head stays on, but their testicles fall off. It's that way with all mammals. Again, we shouldn't interbreed with aliens."

Alien: *(pointing to a pile of bear poop)* "Why do you put all those huckleberries in piles on the trail?"

Ranger: "Sometimes hikers will run out of gorp and go off trail in search of food. Then they get lost. Those berries are a little courtesy we in the Park Service like to extend to hikers who don't carry enough food. This keeps them on the trail and they don't get lost. But even if you're not lost, feel free to help yourself."

Those are *very real questions* asked in Glacier National Park. I did not make them up. But ask yourself: Would a human ever ask such questions. No! Of course not! If a human were to ask those questions, that would make them "stupid questions," and I've been trained enough to know that there is no such thing. No; only a cerebrally challenged space alien race could ask such questions. More importantly, I have proved beyond a shadow of a doubt that my bosses are always right, so I get to keep my job. I think.

Breaking Wind

Many people work for the government because it offers great benefits as compensation for lack of wages. Full-time government employees have a health plan that includes medical, dental, and, if they work with the IRS, a mental plan (necessary for people who actually *desire* to work for the IRS). As a mere seasonal government employee with the Park Service, I work only three months of the year, and so my benefit package is much simpler: nine months of unpaid vacation. Since I can't afford to go on vacation after leaving the park, I just go home to East Glacier, 13 miles away.

Living in East Glacier in winter is wonderful, especially if one is into exploring the nuances of cabin fever. Winter is severe ... lots of snow, bitter temperatures. It is much like winter in Antarctica, except colder and with fewer tourists. But one element that really sets winter in East Glacier apart is the wind. When I say wind, I don't mean those gentle zephyrs known to caress the skin in Great Falls and Livingston. I mean big winds that recently knocked over a train, ripped the roofs off houses, snapped large trees like toothpicks, and obliterated garages and sheds. And during the winter, it blows harder. In other parts of the country, these winds are called "hurricane-force gales," but locals in East Glacier just say, "My, but it's breezy."

These winds are an everyday part of winter life in East Glacier, where the town motto is Every Day Is a Bad Hair Day! In the morning, one can look outside and see small children on their way to school, blowing along like colorful, somersaulting tumbleweeds. Eventually, the children get blown into the school fence, and their little, primary-colored snowsuits get snagged. Teachers, who have some weight and can handle the gale, lean into the wind and harvest the children off the fence, bring them indoors, and begin classes. The school secretary is in charge of driving the streets and collecting the children who had the misfortune of missing the fence and continued their tumbleweed travels toward Cut Bank.

Wind speed indicators, or "enema-monitors," have a very short lifespan in East Glacier. They work for a little while, but then it gets real windy (into triple digits), and they get blown away. One of the more reliable "emu-meateaters" was former-general-store-owner Dick Greenshield's toilet. He put in a new "eeny-minotaur" and noticed that when the wind speed hit 100 miles an hour, the wind howling over his plumbing vents would create pressure changes that caused his toilet to flush. Well, the wind ultimately got his "wind speed thingy," but he could still tell when the wind hit 100 mph, especially when sitting down and enjoying *Reader's Digest.*

Rather than allow this wind to trap me indoors, I have decided to use it for winter recreation. You have probably seen pictures of beautiful, tanned people in warm, tropical climes recreating by using a boat to tow them aloft while they are comfortably harnessed into a parachute. They smile and wave to the oily people on the beaches who sit on towels and wave back. I figured I could do the same without the frills of a beach, boat, or beautiful people; all I needed was the wind and a parachute. March seemed like a good time for the experiment. There's an old cliché regarding the weather in Montana in March: "In like a lion. Out like a butt load of lions."

My wife said it was a horrid idea and that I would get slammed into the ground. But my friends, Chris and Billy Bob, over a few beers, said it sounded brilliant. (Note to self: listen to wife more—and remember that the combination of testosterone and beer can drop an IQ to a dangerously low level.)

The tools required for this little aeronautical adventure were simple: A posthole digger, a four-by-four post, two dollars worth of hardware (including 60 feet of rope), and a parachute purchased on Ebay ("Cheap! Kinda works!"). The plan was to sink the post in a field about half a mile from my house, use the hardware to clip in a carabiner, and then tie the rope to the parachute harness. I'd deploy the chute, the wind would keep me aloft, and I could fly just a few feet off the ground. I figured with the wind, 60 feet of rope would get me about 10 to 15 feet into the air. That was a miscalculation I don't intend to repeat.

During the construction phase, Chris and Billy Bob helped out. Many people in town consider Chris the long lost twin of the supermodel Fabio. Chris looks a lot like him, except more masculine. He's huge and chiseled and has blond hair down to his waist. He always has three days' worth of stubble on his chin, even immediately after shaving. Not many backhoes are as fast as he is with a posthole digger. Good thing, too—the ground was frozen.

Billy Bob came to East Glacier via Arkansas. He speaks with a southern drawl, yet is surprisingly intelligent. He lives off the bounty of the land and dresses in animal skins. A thick, unkempt salt-and-pepper beard obscures 90 percent of his face. People say he looks like Cro-Magnon man and that he lives in a badger hole, which is ridiculous, because I know for a fact that he lives in a rather spacious cave. Many judge Billy Bob using his appearance as their only guide, which is a mistake. Underneath that rough exterior is the heart of a gentle deer—which is all dried up and shriveled and is worn around Billy Bob's neck as a talisman. He is like most of us in many respects, except that he's really different. He's an excellent handyman and it didn't hurt my plan that his best friend runs a hardware store.

Chris dug the hole and sunk the post, while Billy Bob took care of the carriage bolt with the eyehook and carabiner. I prepared the parachute and harness. We were all very serious about this endeavor and, as such, brought lots of beer—just in case.

We were all ready. I gave my friends the thumbs up. Chris and Billy Bob took up strategic positions in lawn chairs on either side of the beer. The air was still by East Glacier standards, or, by normal wind standards, about 35 mph.

The experiment in flight worked flawlessly ... for a while. The chute deployed with an audible "flump!" and I was gently lifted into the air. I was flying! I was soaring effortlessly, like an eagle, just 10 feet off the ground. Within a few seconds I could steer to the left or the right in my tethered flight. It worked! It was as if I was cradled in the hand of God—an angel soaring between heaven and earth. Then the wind speed picked up considerably, and I got closer to heaven than I had planned.

In theory, I was only supposed to be a few feet off the ground. In theory, the post should have stayed anchored, and, in theory, a parachute should have cushioned my landing. The difference between theory and practice can be shocking, if not painful. The wind shifted, and within a few seconds, I went from 10 feet in the air to the full 60 feet. I went straight up over the post. Chris and Billy Bob showed their deep concern by pointing and laughing. I shouted to my friends "Help!" and "Hey! I can see my house from here!" Then the post worked its way out of the ground, and my altitude climbed.

I don't know how many people have witnessed a para-chutist flying through the air with a four-by-four post dangling 60 feet below. I should think it would be quite popular at air shows, judging by the laughter of Chris and Billy Bob. Luckily for me, as I lost altitude, the post and rope got caught in a barbed wire fence. There I was, only moments before cradled in the hand of God, and then the Almighty decided I needed a good Old Testament type of smiting. As the parachute con-tinued to inflate and collapse, I was repeatedly slammed into the ground. Fortunately, after a few minutes my friends caught up to me and pinned me to the ground. They unclipped the parachute harness from the post and stood up. Then the chute inflated again, and I was dragged across the ground. But this time I was unencumbered with the post, so I went a little faster. The wind chill was below freezing, but the friction between the ground and my body kept me plenty warm. I would have been lost for sure, but fortuitously, after a quarter-mile drag, I got caught in the school fence. As the first-grade teacher was freeing me, Chris and Billy Bob came running up. This time, through a process of elimination, they figured out how to remove me from the harness *before* letting go of me again.

It was the happiest trip anyone ever took to a hospital. Chris and Billy Bob recounted what had happened and could almost tell the whole story (as if I weren't there) without breaking into laughter. At the hospital one doctor told me I was lucky it was cold that day and that I was wearing so many protective layers of clothing. It prevented worse cuts, bruises, lacerations, and friction burns. He told me that I would heal, but, alas, he couldn't do much for my IQ. Another doctor told me I was "wacko" and had the worst case of cabin fever he had ever seen. But he was a psychologist and knew next to nothing about treating cuts and bruises. He said the Park Service gave me "way too much free time"—time to get into trouble—and that I should consider a "real" job.

Looking back on the whole parachute escapade, I think the shrink may have been right. Maybe I do have too much free time with nine months off, "idle hands," and all that. Although I love my Park Service job, it's time to look into jobs with real benefits. I'm now applying for a job with the IRS.

I think I should fit in nicely.

Funny Money

Financially, you don't get to where I am overnight. It takes years of wrong turns and bad decisions, not to mention a complete lack of business acumen. I've always been this way. Genetically, I lack the "prosperity" gene, which directly affects my ambition gland and releases apathy into my bloodstream. It makes people like me indifferent toward finances and the means to earn money. The affliction was strongest in my childhood.

Many years ago, prior to the diagnosis, I had a sweet and kind teacher who tried to teach me good old-fashioned values, including lessons regarding money and honest work. When I was in second grade, she set me down on her lap and told me Aesop's fables. You know that old parable, the one with the hard-working ant and the fiddle-playing grasshopper? Well, using that time-honored story, she told me that I would grow up to be just like the drooling wino sprawled out in the alley. What? There's no wino in that story?! Damned teacher!

My personal philosophy about money can be summed up thusly: money, quite simply, is something *other people* have. Lawyers, doctors, pharmacists, and even phlebotomists have money—and I don't know what they are, exactly. Heck, even "year-round" rangers have money ... just not a whole lot (but I did see one with a new car once).

As a seasonal ranger, I don't have money. I have fun, which is just like money, but worthless—at least in terms of its purchasing power. But due to my affliction, I keep a little cliché running through my head, and it always makes me feel better: "Money doesn't buy happiness, it buys Prozac." I don't need Prozac. My job makes me happy.

For almost twenty years, I've been working seasonally for Glacier. Most seasonals are teachers. This arrangement benefits the Park Service greatly because they have an employee with summers off who is already used to very low pay. I've tried teaching, and initially, I had a lot of fun. But then the students showed up, and everything changed. Now, during the winter, I work odd jobs. Odd jobs being defined as, "Look! Hagan's working! That's odd." I chop wood for people and shovel snow off their sidewalks and roofs. I clean office buildings and wash dishes at the diner. Employment in East Glacier, especially in winter, can be tough. Luckily, my family and I have adapted to these financial realities and can subsist for long periods of time by consuming only packing peanuts.

I recently attended my twentieth high school reunion and was much surprised at the conversations my old cronies were having. Actually, everybody was having the same conversation. They were speaking about money. I just listened. I had nothing to add because after almost twenty seasons with the Park Service, all I have to show for it is a multitude of worn-out hiking boots. Everyone was speaking a funny language I didn't understand. And when I say funny, I don't mean strange. They were making me laugh out loud at their gibberish. They spoke in numbers and letters at the same time, speaking about "401Ks" and "401Bs," "portfolios," and "mutual bonds." Then, I heard the funniest financial word of all: "fiduciary." I was sipping a drink as I heard this word, and I thought it was so funny, I shot pink lemonade out both nostrils. Which was kind of weird, since I was drinking beer.

But the long and the short of it was, I realized that I'm running out of time. I mistakenly thought life should be spent doing something you love, something you believe in and are passionate about. I realize now, after hearing my classmates, I was seriously in error. I should have been planning my retirement years ago, building up a nice nest egg. But, alas, I have squandered my time and now I'm between a rock and a hard time. How can I make it through my golden years without consuming food meant for pets? I need to move fast and keep my options open. Due to my genetic defect, I need to come up with nontraditional plans to accumulate wealth quickly. I need a strategy to get me on par financially with my hard working, ant-like friends while taking into account the lack of a prosperity gene.

So I have sat down and brainstormed (fantasized) about work possibilities that offer the most bang for the buck. Again, these may not seem "normal," by most standards, but I'm not "normal" by any standard I'm aware of.

First on my list of jobs I'd like is "Letter Turner." Someday, Vanna White will retire from Wheel of Fortune or at least take a stress break from the rigors of her labor. That's where I can step in. I can picture myself at the interview (insert wavy dream lines here).

Interviewer: "So, Mr. Hagan, can you turn letters?"
Me: "I can turn consonants and vowels. And, though I've never tried, I bet I can do hyphens and ampersands too."

Interviewer: "I see" *(makes notes on yellow legal pad).* "How are you at clapping enthusiastically?"
Me: "Clapping? You bet, I could be a regular cheerleader."

Interviewer: "Do you have a great smile?"
Me: "Well, I could with the help of a good oral surgeon."

Interviewer: "Do you look great in a dress?" *(One eyebrow goes way up.)*
Me: "Um ... well ..." *(eyes shifting)* "Yes, I have this red strapless number" *(now making eye contact and seeing both eyebrows go up and down in unison).* "It's hot!"

Interviewer: "Get the hell out of my office!"

On second thought, maybe I should think about being a game show host. Or maybe a movie star. Movie stars make a lot of money. I wouldn't even have to move out to Hollywood; I could stay in East Glacier if I were a movie star. Lots of Block Buster movies have been made in Glacier because of its stunning scenery. Take *The Lord of the Rings* trilogy, for example, all those jagged snowcapped mountains and glaciated valleys—that's New Zealand, but it sure looks like Glacier—and those movies were huge successes. Next on our example list is *Heaven's Gate*, which was filmed in Glacier and widely thought to be the worst movie ever made. I've actually seen a small part of this movie, and I can tell you, even that little bit was too much. But other movies have been filmed in Glacier: *The Shining, Beethoven's 2nd, What Dreams May Come.*

I once met an actor who had worked in Glacier. I don't want to name names in this day and age of contingency fee lawyers, so to preserve his anonymity, I'll just call him "Mr. Large Island Off the Coast of Florida." Well, "Mr. Large Island Off the Coast of Florida" owes me money and hasn't paid up. He came into my wife's diner, where some of my photographs were on display. While I was doing dishes, he was admiring my photos. He said he liked them, and I (maybe too eagerly) jumped on an opportunity. "They're for sale," I said and in short order had closed an order for about three or four matted and shrink-wrapped photos. I sent the photos and an invoice, and he never paid up. "Mr. Large Island Off the Coast of Florida's" business partner even called to apologize for not paying and said I would have a check soon. It didn't come. After about a year of correspondence, I just gave up. But now with interest, I figure, those photos are worth nearly $4 gazillion dollars. So, show me the money, "Mr. Large Island Off the Coast of Florida." Meanwhile, I'm coming up with other schemes that allow a cushy retirement.

I know! I could be an inventor! I've got this great idea. You know how some women use fake nails? It's true. They use press-on nails. These nails are plastic, but they look just like real nails, unless you tap them on the countertop; then you know they are fake because of the odd sound they make. But my idea is for men and men only. (At this point, women must quit reading.) I've even done a commercial (insert wavy dream lines here).

Gentlemen, aren't you tired of being dragged to Brad Pitt movies? Do you hate men's health magazines like *Better Abs and Sex?* Do you hate the spare tire around your middle? Are you afraid to walk shirtless on beaches because of that weirdo with a wooden leg and a harpoon? Well, now you can relax. We have a solution! Hagan's Press-On Abs! Yes, you can have rippling abs with no effort at all. Simply smear the sticky goop and press that washboard six-pack on! It looks so real! Just listen to this testimonial:

Babe: "I used to find my husband visually repugnant. But now that he has press-on abs, I'll hold his hand ... sometimes."

Man: "Thank you, press-on abs! (slurps beer and shoves pork rinds into his face.) Yes, these press-on abs are the perfect solution to your flabby middle. No sit-ups, crunches, or anything. Just press them on and be careful not to bump into countertops, or everyone will know your abs are fake. Real abs don't click."

Um ... maybe I shouldn't be an inventor. I should probably save my money and do some responsible investing, like buying lottery tickets. I know what you're thinking: no one from Montana, let alone a tiny town of 300 people like East Glacier, is ever going to win the lottery. HA! WRONG! Someone from East Glacier already *did* win the lottery! Really! Yes, acquaintances of mine walked away with almost 20 million dollars! So, it's not unprecedented; East Glacier has already had winners! Um ... so ... I guess the chances of another lottery winner from the same small town ... are ... come to think of it ... astronomically small. So maybe I shouldn't buy lottery tickets. Oh, heck, maybe I'll just move somewhere else in Montana and that will make my odds ... only slightly better.

I might be able to retire if I exploit my kids. They're both beautiful children, and people always tell me that they got all my good looks, which I guess is true—since my wife still has hers. They are both smart, cute, and talented. Emma, my daughter, can sing like an angel; she's a brilliant actress; and she's quite gifted musically and can play piano by ear. (I wish she'd use her fingers; she just bangs her head on the keyboard. But it sounds very nice.) Leo, my little boy, is about as cute as can be. He had dimples deep enough to pot a geranium in and a smile that could melt the polar icecaps (actually, that's probably why they're melting). Somebody, somewhere, will recognize *their* talents and offer *me* huge, vast sums of money. Isn't that how exploitation is supposed to work? Of course, I love my kids. It would be nice if they loved me back—maybe I shouldn't exploit them. Maybe, all on their own, they have enough talent to make it rich. Then, maybe, they'll give me some.

Maybe I should just try to be an example for my kids. Make an effort, try hard, and I might be a success. It seems to work for everyone else. I should forget all my harebrained retirement schemes. Hard work is its own reward. Dang it! This is America, and we can all make money and retire comfortably if we try hard. It's all about initiative, industry, and creativity. Anyone who puts forth the effort will be rewarded. As for me, I'm going to write while I'm not "rangering" around in the woods. If I make a real honest effort at writing, I might reap honest financial rewards. I have already thought of a great pen name to help me reach my retirement goals: "Stephen King."

Freezer Burn

It was a dark and stormy night, because when you want to establish a creepy mood, it's always a dark and stormy night. Lightning crashes, you grow more tense, and then a black cat meows really loudly. Chilling, huh? An ominous heartbeat is heard in the background. I'm a little freaked out! I'm getting out of this frightening introduction and moving on to the next paragraph.

Who knows what evil lurks in the hearts of men? Ask the Shadow's nose. And if you were to ask that big, dark nose about me, he'd tell you not to look into my chest freezer. But just as in all horror stories, you wouldn't listen. Admit it. You're kind of goofy that way. You'd go snooping, just like my sister, Malady.

My chest freezer is quite large; about 4 feet long by 2 feet wide and 3 feet deep. You could easily stuff a human body in there ... maybe two or three. But *I've* got about fifty or more bodies, plus a dog leg and a bunch of brains, some still in their skulls. (More lightning–ohhh!)

It all started innocently enough. I was only trying to help. But then things spiraled out of control. It's not my fault. I was driven to this madness by my friend Eric and my students. They're the ones that turned me into Dr. Evil. (Muahahaha.)

I have always been fascinated with animals. As a kid I wanted to be a veterinarian. I used to picture myself in surgical garb in the doggy delivery room, saying to the proud mother, "Congratulations! It's octuplets—and they're mutts." I would have been a great vet, but then I learned how hard they worked, so I had to look into other fields of employment. But the childhood fascination with animals didn't go away. I still stop for roadkill, and if it's in good shape, I keep it. But I didn't just snap one day and start stuffing human bodies in my freezer—that would be too much like Postal Service employees. I'm with the Park Service, so relax. And I've only stuffed one human body in my freezer.

My freezer issue evolved slowly. Because I was a science teacher and a ranger, children would wind up on my porch with a bird who had smacked into their window or a chipmunk who had lost a game of dodge-paw with a cat. These children wanted to help in any way they could, and in their desperation, they turned to me, which should tell you how desperate they really were. Young impressionable children think their science teachers know everything—because that's what I *taught them to think*. But surely a science teacher masquerading as a ranger would be able to help these poor woodland creatures. Unfortunately, more of these perished than prospered. So into my freezer they went, destined to become future taxidermy projects.

Now, before someone gets their underwear in a bunch, which someone always does when the subject of treating injured birds comes up, let me explain that federal law prohibits just anyone picking up birds, dead or alive, and providing help, especially to the dead ones. The Feds are a persnickety bunch, and they don't want your help with injured birds unless you've filled out the necessary paperwork, in triplicate, and filed it with the Federal Department of Redundancy Department Bureau.

For example, I once came across a golden eagle with a broken wing. I called the proper federal officials with the location of the bird, mile marker, and so on, and told them I'd wait there to keep the majestic bird from walking out onto the interstate and becoming majestic bird paste.

After approximately two hours of waiting, I made up "plan B." Since the officials I had called didn't show up, I called my ornithology professor, who, while getting his Ph.D. in birds (of all things), handled and banded large birds of prey, such as eagles.

Because he wasn't working for an hourly wage, my professor came out right away. He brought with him some very sophisticated, high-tech bird of prey capturing equipment: a cardboard box and a blanket. He simply threw the blanket over the bird, which magically calmed the bird—like a sedative. I suspect there was lithium or thorazine in the blanket, but I never asked. Once it was covered, we simply scooped the bird up and placed it in the cardboard box and drove to a veterinarian's office. Simple as that.

After all was said and done, I thought it only polite to call the Feds and tell them that the injured bird had been rescued and was resting comfortably at the animal clinic. Over the phone they said, "Stay *right* there." I naively assumed they were going to present me with a plaque with the word "Hero" engraved with large letters. Maybe they would give me a box of chocolates or some cash to reward me for the rescue. They might even throw confetti.

Boy, was I wrong.

The Fed got out of the car, tugging at his backside (apparently his underwear was creeping up on him), came over to me, and gave me a chewing out I won't soon forget. He didn't throw confetti; he threw a fit. He berated me up one side and down the other with the spit-flying, finger-thumping-the-chest type of yelling. I'm not kidding. So, just FYI, unless you have the proper paperwork filed, don't help injured birds. You heartless bastards. (Oh, go ahead and help—just call a licensed rehabilitator—it will be our little secret.)

Because of my successes treating injured critters (I've had failures, too, but we won't go there), I got a call from Dan the Bear Man, who works for the Blackfeet tribe. He had a grounded hawk and wanted me to have a look. He brought the bird to my house, and I quickly diagnosed a concussion. I could tell it was a concussion by the animated stars orbiting the bird's head.

Normally, when I encounter a bird with this type of injury, I place it in the oven at 350 degrees and take them out when I can wiggle a drumstick. Just kidding. Fixing this bird was too much for me alone. Steroids were needed to reduce swelling, and since there were no professional athletes in East Glacier, steroids were hard to come by—and meth wouldn't do the trick.

I contacted a man in the Swan Valley, Ken, who does nothing but treat injured birds. I made arrangements to drive two hours and hand the bird over to Ken, who was better equipped and infinitely more knowledgeable in avian concussions.

Since it wasn't my first dealing with Ken, he listed me as a "branch office" on his permit. As such, he gave me two ziplock bags, each a gallon and chock-full of little white mice, in case I ever need to feed another injured raptor. So that explains about 99 percent of the lifeless bodies in my freezer: mice.

You may be wondering about the deer heads, brains, and dog leg in my freezer. I'm not into exotic cuisine, so how do I explain them? Again, I'm innocent and misunderstood. I'm guilty only of having a big heart (in my chest, not my freezer).

I have an unusual friend, the aforementioned Eric. Eric took all his money and bought some land just outside East Glacier. After buying the land, he had no money left over for a house, so he lived year-round in a tent with his best friend Quanah, a malamute.

Like everywhere else in the northern latitudes, East Glacier is blessed with the four seasons: Almost Winter, Winter, Still Winter, and Construction. Eric lived in a tent through that whole cycle, and his heat was largely provided à la malamute. Like a tongue to a frosty pole, Eric and Quanah were insepa-rable. They had a bond stronger than superglue.

Eric made his living tanning hides the old way. Just like the Native Americans, Eric would scrape a hide, smear it and soak it in brains, and then smoke it. It's back-breaking work, and Eric earned just enough to pay the taxes on the land and keep a tent over his head. As is often the case with tents, Eric's didn't have electric outlets, so he didn't have a freezer in which he could keep his brains ... for tanning, I mean. So I kept his brains for him. Some were encased as nature intended—still in the deer's head: fur, ears, eyes, tongue, nose, the whole shebang. As needed, Eric and Quanah would come into town, grab some brains/skulls from my freezer and head back to work the hides.

It was a routine that lasted many years. Sadly, over time, Quanah developed cancer in his leg, and Eric just couldn't put his best friend down. He had the leg amputated. Furthermore, Eric knew Quanah didn't have long to live, and it was his wish that when Quanah shuffled off this mortal coil, that he be buried whole—*with* his amputated leg. So, as a favor, I tossed the dog leg in with the deer heads. All were neatly wrapped in clear garbage bags.

So, in my freezer, I've got lots of bodies (mice) and body parts (deer heads and the odd dog leg). It might seem unusual, but you must keep in mind that this is East Glacier. Unusual is the norm. In East Glacier, we all have a good laugh at normal people; they're fun to watch. But imagine someone from the outside world visiting East Glacier. Someone who doesn't spell culture with a capital "k." Someone who isn't hip to East Glacier's lower, weirder standards. If a normal person were to look into my freezer, she might be shocked, even horrified. But as yet no normal person has looked; just my abnormally nervous sister, Malady (oohh, there goes that lightning again).

In East Glacier, we say that there are nine months of winter and three months of relatives (and construction). When

Malady came for a visit, the weather was hot! She should have been used to it because she lives in Florida, where the heat and humidity combination is a one-two punch that could knock anyone out, or at least send them crawling for an iced tea. Malady should have been stronger. It was only 90-plus degrees that day, and, as we like to say in East Glacier, "It's not the heat, it's the humanity."

My marginally insulated house was like a brick kiln, and outside was worse. Poor, frail Malady was the houseguest who couldn't move. She just lay on the couch sweating. Occasionally, unsteady legs carried her from the couch to the fridge, where she'd pour herself some orange juice. Then back to the couch, where she'd collapse. As she'd lie there, I'd try to cheer her up by reading Edgar Allan Poe's "Cask of Amontillado." An odd selection for midday reading, perhaps, but I believe in foreshadowing. Additionally, Malady and I have an understanding: She thinks I'm crazy, and I think she's not far off the mark. That's why I live in East Glacier.

Malady finished a whole pitcher of juice and wanted more. I figured I had done enough for her by reading horror stories, so I very politely said, "Get off your tush and get it yourself." So on wobbly legs, she stood up and made for my chest freezer.

Big mistake.

Malady opened the lid of the chest freezer. Cold, misty air swirled and slowly cleared. Malady bent over for a closer inspection. Inches away, lifeless deer eyes stared back at her through clear plastic. The shrieking violins from *Psycho* began to play. Already weakened by the heat, the shock of seeing bags of mice, a dog leg, and the unmoving eyes of deer staring blankly up at her sent her over the edge with a hard shove. She screamed her best Janet Leigh scream and collapsed.

Upon hearing the scream, I laughed my butt ... I mean, I went to help her in any way I could. There she was, sprawled out on the floor with her eyes rolled back into her head. I felt her forehead. She was burning up with fever.

Having once almost passed a first aid class, I knew she needed to cool off right away. So very gently, I lifted her and put her in the first cool spot I saw: the chest freezer. Then, very kindly, mind you, I placed a soothing, cool bag of mice on her head. A bond formed instantly between the sweat and the frozen bag, and it stuck. Her head tilted just a bit, so that she was eyeball-to-eyeball with a deer head. But that wasn't really a concern. I thought Malady might cool off more quickly if I closed the top of the chest freezer. It was just as the lid was coming down that she regained consciousness.

I have to say, in all modesty, that this method of resuscitation may well earn me a Nobel Prize in medicine. It worked like a charm! In fact, it worked so well, the laws of physics were temporarily suspended. For example, gravity, usually a constant, discontinued during Malady's recovery. There she was, suspended like the law of gravity itself above the chest freezer. I would have thought with the added weight of the deer head she was clutching, not to mention the bag of frozen mice on her head, that hovering would have been difficult, if not impossible. I suspect the hovering action was due to the force generated by her frantically twirling legs. I didn't really have time to study it much because I was preoccupied protecting my eardrums from the banshee shrieks coming from

Malady. I'm sure these screams would have broken glass, but then again, the laws of physics were disabled.

Had I a high-speed camera, the same ones used to film bullets piercing apples, I'm positive I could have documented Malady using "force of will" to get away from the freezer. The camera undoubtedly would have captured her breaking down to a molecular level as she willed herself out of this situation. But, alas, I have no such camera. All I experienced was a thunderclap as air slammed into the vacuum her body had vacated. One second she was there; the next she was gone. I just stood there watching the deer head she dropped rolling back and forth on the floor.

You would think that a woman running at the speed of sound with a bag of frozen mice attached to her head would stand out. But not in East Glacier. It was just weird enough that none of the locals took notice. Malady was perfectly emotionally camouflaged for this town. She raced about with advanced stealth technology, or it's possible that she was just too fast. I later received a call from the highway patrol. They found her running down the highway, cited her for speeding, and wanted me to come and pick her up.

After getting her out of lockdown, I put her in the car and told her that we would look back on this whole thing and laugh; hell, I was already laughing. I said it was an experience we would treasure. Malady wasn't laughing. Her eyes burned with their own evil fire. I swear I heard the shrieking violins from *Psycho* again. She attacked. I don't know how many of you have been bludgeoned with a frozen bag of mice, but it hurts, bad.

The Season's End

I have always claimed that Glacier National Park is the home for my soul. Years of hiking, exploring, and just plain old looking around have taught me that something deep inside me is more alive when I'm inside the park's boundaries. I have a number of "self-images," and one, "Pat Hagan, Ranger Naturalist," is my favorite. That is the person I'd like to be all the time. For example, "Pat Hagan, Ranger Naturalist" is much more fun than "Pat Hagan, Viewer of Bills Marked Past Due." Ranger Naturalist is alive and curious, and he's much funnier than I am. He's the person I'd like to be all the time, and I would be him more often if I could get more work in the park. If I had more work and thus more money, I could kiss the "Viewer of Bills Marked Past Due" goodbye.

Looking back on all the park work, I was toying with the wording of "nineteen years of public service" and had to laugh at myself. The words "public service" have some connotations of self-sacrifice and low pay, neither of which is true in my case. "Public service" implies that I've given my services to the park and to the visiting public, with no thought of myself. And, honestly, the pay isn't bad either. The truth of it is, I've given nothing. The park is the "giver," and I feed off the park like some frail, starving hummingbird off a colorful flower's nectar. I sip its sweetness, deeply, and let it fill me with life and love until I feel flushed with all it has to offer. I'm drawn by its beauty, lured again and again, to sip and saturate myself ... to saturate my soul. "Public service?" No, I come to the park and take from it much more than I have ever given. I'm so lucky to work and live here.

I'm lucky because, when I put on the uniform and go to work in the park, there is no denying that I feel my spirit lift and I'm so much closer to the Creator. I view the peaks as His handiwork, and the flowing water as the essence of life itself. With the Continental Divide running through the park, it would not be an exaggeration to say that water, the source of life, starts in Glacier. Some water flows west to the Pacific Ocean, some east to the Atlantic Ocean, and some even goes north up into Hudson Bay. But the most pure elements of life are at its source of origin, within the park.

I love to get off-trail. The explorer within me loves the unpredictable that comes with getting off the beaten path. The "path" in many ways represents the norm, the safe, the unsurprising. In my line of work as a naturalist, I have to keep the park visitors safe and help them stay on the path. There have been a few times when I've felt adventurous and have led a group with more than a normal share of verve off-trail. But 99.9 percent of the time, I'm on the trail, walking by rocks and roots I've walked by a thousand times before. Seasonally, the flowers may change from glacier lilies to fireweed, but flowers have never been my benchmarks. Items moored more permanently, like roots and rocks and some trees, are the ones who greet me, say "hello," time and time again, as I walk the familiar paths.

Sometimes (it doesn't happen often, but it happens) no one shows up for a scheduled hike. There I am at the trailhead at the prearranged time and date with no company, no one with which to go hiking ... just me. I love it. No one shows up, and I have the options of just going home or back to the ranger station, taking a nap, or reading a book. But I don't recall ever going home or back to the ranger station, even in the rain. I go for a hike all alone, and frequently I go off-trail. The starving hummingbird again sipping at the flower's nectar. I go in search of adventure and that feeling of connection, a direct union between my soul and the Creator. (I hope readers will not be thinking that I'm trying to write some prose that strives for the divine and falls hopelessly short. Worse than that, they may think I'm false. But I have a feeling some readers, especially the dyed-in-the-wool lovers of Glacier, will recognize this sentiment. They will understand it because they have experienced it; they too have made the connection— and it isn't false. Not one bit.)

As I walk alone, I'm often talking to the Almighty. He's never talked back, but I figure He's a good listener. I usually ask Him to watch over my wife and kids and watch over my Dad, who is dealing with a multitude of health issues. I ask for help with my father-in-law's systemic cancer. I ask him to help ailing friends: Pat's fibromyalgia, Doug's headaches ... and I ask that the spots on Mike's x-rays just turn out to be benign shadows. I ask Him to help me on a personal level. I ask for guidance on how to be a more patient parent and husband. I ask, "What is my calling? What am I to do with my life?" (I figure He has a sense of humor regarding that one.) And I ask Him to keep me safe, since I am hiking solo that day. Solo hiking is the time for me to chat with the Almighty. I can't do it leading a group. I'm bound to generate some complaints and give everyone the impression that I'm nuts—or at least, nuttier than I am.

Logan Pass is one of my least favorite places in the Park during June, July, and August. It's beautiful but just too crowded for my taste. But after Labor Day, the steady stream of visitors is reduced to a trickle, and each day that follows, the trickle becomes less and less. By mid-October the spigot is just about shut off. The 2003 season will long be remembered as a hot one. Multiple fires brought their changes to the forests of the west side of the park, and because of all the press the fires were generating, the number of visitors to the park went way down. One good thing about the fires was that Congress was reminded about Glacier National Park. In an attempt to help bring more visitors, they threw money our way, the Going to the Sun road remained open well into the middle of October and my season was extended.

October has some variable weather, but I believe there is no such thing as bad weather, just bad clothing. The very last day the road was open, I had the pleasure of working up at

Logan Pass. The visitor center had been boarded up, all its books moved out, and the flies swept off the windowsills. Many other naturalists drove up to the pass and dispensed information and answered questions while sitting in the car. I could never do that. No matter the weather, I couldn't be confined to the car. I'd grab a shovel and clear snow from the steps or level off the snowdrift on the trail around Clement's Moraine. You'd be surprised at how many visitor contacts or questions you get, shoveling a mile and a half of trail. It's my belief that it's more than you'd get in a car, anyway.

As I arrived at Logan Pass, there was only one car in the parking lot—a new gold Subaru Forester with Lake County license plates. There was a sticker on the back indicating that the driver was in the service, a chopper flier. It was the only car I saw that day. The trickle of visitors had been shut off. It was the last day the road would be open. Due to a big accumulation of snow and its subsequent melt-off and refreezing, the superintendent had said "enough." The Going to the Sun Road would close the following day. Besides, the additional money was all but gone.

I arrived at the pass around 9:30 in the morning. It was cold, but I was dressed for it. The day was cloudy and calm, not a breath of wind, which made the pass unusually quiet and tranquil. I hung out near the steps leading to the visitor center for hours. The cold was creeping into my body through my vibram soles. I'd stomp my feet, trying to get feeling back into my toes. I needed to generate some heat; I needed to move. Cold, wanderlust, and boredom hit simultaneously, and off I went, not sure where my feet would take me.

As it turned out, my feet wanted to go to Hidden Lake, but took the long way. I'd keep looking back toward the parking lot, but no more cars were coming that day. Logan Pass was, for all intents and purposes, closed. The wind had picked up slightly, and the icicles hanging from the fir trees began to clink softly up against one another.

The mountains had an otherworldly appearance that day, and I don't know that it can be accurately described. To tell of their appearance, you have to understand the weather during the previous days. First, a day of saturating rain. Then, about 6 inches of heavy, wet snow that quickly melted. Then, a cold freeze. All this gave the mountains a veneer I'd never seen before, and I'd be surprised to ever see it again. Where once waterfalls filled in all the crags, there was now ice. On ledges, the ice formed miniature dams and caused the flowing water to come off in a level even sheet, which then froze. It looked as though the mountains were coated in a layer of translucent plastic or melted, dripping candle wax.

I went down to the bottom of the valley and worked my way through the ice-covered fir trees to a lake that my friend, Rick, and I named "Epiphany Lake." I guess, technically, it's part of Hidden Lake, but it rests 30 to 50 vertical feet above the bigger lake, with Bear Hat Mountain rising sharply above it to the west. The unusual thing about this small lake is its outlet. Where the water pours out of the lake is just like the lip of a pitcher or carafe. If you had constructed a wall of clay and simply pinched and pulled out a small section, that is what the outlet is like. You can straddle the outlet, and if you chose to, you could jump into Epiphany Lake from that very spot and be in over your head in crystal clear, icy water. I had done it before, but not today. On a warm day, the water is chilly enough to crush testicles. Today, both the air and the water temperatures were too low, and jumping in would be slow suicide by hypothermia. If the water didn't get you, the exposure to the air would.

Walking away from the noise of the outlet toward the head of Hidden Lake, I started to hear new, unfamiliar sounds. Normally, when I'm down in that area alone, I think the noise I would most likely hear is the "woof" of a grizzly. The noise I actually heard was far from a "woof." It was mixture of sounds: the gentle clinking of champagne glasses, a chime of a bell, crunching of rocks, and thunder. Fragments of the "dripped wax," the ice shells, were beginning to thaw and break off the mountains. In the past, I've heard avalanches come down in the spring. I've heard lots, not that they are common to my ear. They didn't sound like this new sound at all.

When an avalanche lets fly, tons of snow and rock tumble down upon sound-insulating snow and rock at the valley bottom. It is thunderous, like a low-flying jet. This day was ice and rock. No muted sounds caused by the padded layers of snow, no muffling of the breaking of the crystals. A totally new sound: champagne glasses, chimes, rocks, and thunder.

I walked to the very head of Hidden Lake; if there was a path to the spot in which I ended, I didn't take it. I pulled my lunch out of my pack and scanned the ice upon the Dragon's Tail, a mountain enclosing the head of Hidden Lake. As the day wore on, it grew only slightly warmer. Occasionally a shaft of yellow-gold light would penetrate, but it was mostly just a gray, overcast day. I sat, ate jerky, and listened. You could count on shards of ice to come down about every fifteen seconds or so.

The ringing of the ice as it fell off the mountains on to the rocks below was mesmerizing. A couple of times, the ice or a rock would make a high, zippy sound like the ricochet of a bullet, but by far my favorite was when it hit the water. It only hit twice that I recall, but the end of the chiming, icy symphony came with a deep bass "Ka-thuppp" as the larger pieces hit the water. It was awesome.

Alone, listening to the new thunder at the water's edge, I started to talk to God, as I so often do. My heart was full to bursting, and I thanked him for a day unlike any day I had previously experienced in all my years. This day didn't sound or look like any prior: mountains dipped in shattering wax. I expressed gratitude for a job that got me outside and put me in high spirits so often. I thanked Him for wild lands and wolverines, grizzlies, glaciers, and all things truly wild. I thanked Him for putting me on the planet, my health, and all the people I have met along the trail. I thanked Him for the water seeping into my old leather boots. I thanked him for warm feet. I thanked Him for all I could think of—all of it, everything.

Eventually I had to leave my private Eden. I stuffed my lunch back into my backpack, threw it over my shoulders, and headed back along the trail. This day was so special, so unique, because alone I had experienced the mountains' crying song. But in being alone, I couldn't actually, truly, share the experience. Beauty is a secret best shared. You have to be there. Sure, I'd tell the people about the mountains' icy veneer and the crashing of ice racing toward the valley bottom, the crystal, chiming sound of ice on rock, or the bass notes as ice hit water. But to truly understand, you had to be there, and in that regard I was alone. I hiked back toward the parking lot.

Toward the top of the trail, I sat on a rock. I looked down at the lake and across at the mountains. What a difference a few hours made. The place looked more ... normal. Most of the ice had fallen, and the mountains took on their usual wet, dark stony appearance. As I sat, I heard a faint "Hey, Bear!" shouted from far down below. I watched a party of five start the assent from the lake. I sat for twenty minutes or so until they got to my level.

It turned out they were a hiking club: three men and two women. I recall they were from Lakeside and Polson and judging from their age I assumed them to be part of the "Over the Hill Gang." But no, just a small group of enthusiastic, adventurous hikers. They had gone toward Floral Park over the pass between Bear Hat and the Dragon's Tail and called it a day. As we continued the climb out toward the trailhead I cautiously asked one of the men, "Did you guys hear that ice falling off the cliffs?"

"Yeah, that was something else, wasn't it! Never heard anything like it!" He had been a chopper pilot in the army. Drove a Subaru.

Now I had someone to share it with—a new connection. What a great way to close out a season. We walked toward the parking lot, and the wind and rain started to pick up.

I said my goodbyes, got into my car, and headed downhill toward St. Mary. The Subaru went the other way toward West Glacier. I drove a couple of miles and kept checking my rearview mirror, trying to get a last look at Logan Pass. I went through the tunnel and was forced to use one of the pullouts just on the other side. I wasn't done. My season wasn't over yet; there was one more thing. I got out of the car and looked back at Logan Pass. Wind and water whipped my face.

"Thanks again," I whispered. Even with the wind, I think He heard.